CHRISTIAN BROTHERHOOD:

A

LETTER

TO THE

HON. HEMAN LINCOLN.

BY

BARON STOW, D.D.,

PASTOR OF THE ROWE-STREET CHURCH, BOSTON.

BOSTON:
GOULD AND LINCOLN,
59 WASHINGTON STREET.
NEW YORK: SHELDON AND COMPANY.
CINCINNATI: GEORGE S. BLANCHARD.
1859.

ELECTROTYPED BY

W. F. DRAPER, ANDOVER, MASS.

PRINTED BY

GEO. C. RAND & AVERY, BOSTON.

CONTENTS.

CHRISTIAN BROTHERHOOD.

TO THE HONORABLE HEMAN LINCOLN:

MY DEAR CHRISTIAN BROTHER,—

As I have a few thoughts upon an important subject which I wish to convey, in a familiar manner, to those Christian disciples by whose distinctive name we are both known, and to whom we sustain endeared relations, I venture respectfully to avail myself of the influence of your name as a valuable aid to their transmission.

I can think of no fitter medium. For nearly sixty years you have been attached by profession and by practice to the people called Baptists, and during that period you have never wavered from the great principles on which their churches have ever been "grounded and settled." Having been led to the cross for pardon, and introduced into the "household of faith," by that eminent servant of God, whose memory is so fragrant in our American Zion, the Rev. Dr. Baldwin; and having enjoyed, through many years, not only the benefits of his instructive ministry, but the peculiar advantages of a confidential intimacy which death only could interrupt, you had the best of facilities for acquiring a thorough knowledge of Divine truth, and becoming intelligently established in those doctrines which are the believer's rock of strength. The result has been seen in your history, which, by the grace of God, has been happily protracted. You are understood to be now, at fourscore, what you was previous to your majority — a Baptist. As such, you are widely known, and as widely respected. Though you have out-lived whole generations, and though nearly all who knew you best have gone to their final home, yet the name of no other layman in our ecclesiastical connection is to-day familiar to so many ears, and dear to so many hearts, as the name you bear.

But it is not merely or chiefly the estimation in which you are held that prompts me to associate with your name this particular service. Having, for more than thirty years, been favored with your personal friendship, and also, as I believe, with your fraternal confidence, I have had ample opportunity to become acquainted with your opinions and feelings with respect to every question that pertains to the Christian Life and the advancement of the Redeemer's kingdom. We have often conversed upon the evil of schisms among the friends of Christ, and the desirableness of some cordial, successful endeavor to bring nearer together the divided portions of that Body of which Christ is the Head; and I understand that your views, and those which may find expression in this Letter, are essentially coincident. I know not the particular in which we have ever disagreed; and the fact that our Christian sympathies have run so long and so concurrently in a common channel, has contributed largely to the pleasure of my ministry. However the advocates of a relaxed carefulness in Christian morals may have regarded you as exact and scrupulous, you have never, I am sure, been charged with anything like narrowness or exclusiveness in your love to the great Christian brotherhood. Immovably as you have rested upon the fundamental truths of Divine Revelation, as you understand them, and firmly as you have adhered to the ecclesiastical polity which you believe to be developed in the New Testament, the discovery of the first indication of sectarian bigotry is reserved for the man who has not yet appeared. The right of private judgment — that primary principle dear to every consistent Baptist — I have never known you to question, either directly or by implication. You have been accustomed to respect the consciences of others just as you would have your own conscience respected. While you have been compelled by assured convictions to occupy essentially the platform of a sect, yet, as fitting occasions have offered, you have never failed to rise superior to that platform, and occupy the higher, broader plane of Christian fraternity, manifesting your fellowship with multitudes not included in your own denomination. Your special connection with a people of a particular name, you have never felt to be a bondage. Your comprehensive brotherly love has found, in numerous ways, unrestricted scope. You have desired no greater freedom than you have uniformly enjoyed; and of the privileges of a free Christian you have, at pleasure, availed yourself, ever mindful of all Divine limitations, ever having respect to "the perfect Law of liberty." Hence you have been accustomed, during a long life, not only to associate on equal terms with Christians of other names, but also to coöperate with them in works of benevolence. This has been your delight; and it has given you a wide-spread influence, conciliating thousands, not only towards yourself as liberal, but also towards the denomination whose spirit you represented. In reviewing the past from your present position on the frontier of the Better Land, you do not, I am confident, regret that you have cherished, on so broad a scale, this spirit, adding to your "brotherly-kindness charity," or that you have given to this feeling of your heart so varied and distinct an expression. Assuredly, your eternal future is brightened by the prospect of association with many whom you have known here, not as Baptists, but as Christians, — the redeemed by the blood of our Saviour.

Some personal explanations, at this point, may not be impertinent. While on a journey to New York, in the autumn of 1842, I had a seat for several hours by the side of a clergyman of another denomination, whom I had long known as a devoted Christian, and for whom I cherished a strong fraternal affection. We had labored together in efforts for the spiritual benefit of our fellow-men, and on almost every point of Christian truth and duty our views had ever been in delightful harmony. Our conversation, during those hours of spiritual communion, turned mainly upon prayer as a means of promoting personal holiness, and more particularly upon the idea suggested by the words of the apostle — "supplication for all saints." As an illustration of his own views, my excellent brother mentioned the happy effect upon his own mind of a practical compliance with that suggestion. His words were: "I have been a happier man ever since I adopted the practice of always praying for other denominations before I pray for my own, or even for myself. My heart has been drawn out, as it never was before, in love for all Christians. I now know what it is to sympathize in their afflictions and rejoice in their prosperity, and they all seem to me as my Father's family." These remarks were lodged in my memory, and became the subject of many reflections, and the occasion of some tender emotions. A few months afterwards, being disqualified, by the loss of my voice, for public labor, I availed myself of the silence and solitude to which I was subjected, to do what I never could have accomplished amid the activities of my pastoral vocation, — I put upon paper the substance of the following communication. The manuscript has remained in my hands more than fifteen years, — a period much longer than Horace recommends to authors for purposes of revision and emendation. The whole has been since rewritten with as much of care as was compatible with multiplied public duties. You will perceive that I have not confined myself to a development of the germinal thought, — prayer for all Christians,

— but I have taken a much broader range, and introduced that thought as one of a series.

I have adopted the epistolary, rather than the didactic or the declamatory, style, as possessing some peculiar advantages, especially as being the more familiar and affectionate mode of address, and adapted to the present condition of my moral feelings.

That my views will meet from all a cordial assent, I do not, of course, anticipate. Still, I venture the expectation that by many they will be kindly welcomed; for I am sure that, in our denomination, there are thousands in whose bosoms is a sympathetic chord that ever vibrates at the lightest touch of this tender subject, — thousands who are inquiring for some path in which they can legitimately and honestly walk towards a consummation for which their hearts are ever longing. To all such I would gladly render some aid; and in the attempt I trust it will not appear that I assume the office of censor, or even of teacher. My desire is to suggest, without a breach of modesty, such considerations as may possibly facilitate thought and activity in the desirable direction. Should the effort contribute in any measure towards the accomplishment of its intended object, I shall be grateful to Him to whom I regard myself as indebted, both for

2

the motive by which it has been prompted, and for the Spirit under whose guidance it has been conceived and executed.

You, my brother, understand me, and will be apprehensive of no sinister design, on my part, to remove any of the ancient land-marks. And yet your observation has taught you how possible it is that I may be suspected of a tendency to diverge from the "old paths," and a disposition to sacrifice truth upon the altar of theory.[1] You are aware of no such proclivity. "I dwell among mine own people." From convictions formed in early life, and often since reviewed, I am conscientiously one of them, and one with them. I know not that I have ever felt or exhibited antipathy to any denomination of Christians. I have seen excellences in all, such as we might profitably imitate, and I have never seen the hour when I was not perfectly willing, should my investigations touching the correctness of our belief and practice make the duty obvious, to change my ecclesiastical name and relations, and unite with any portion of "the household of

[1] "Commonly, it brings a man under suspicion of favoring some heresy, or abating his zeal, if he but attempt a pacificatory work."—*Baxter's Reformed Pastor.*

faith," where truth might appear to be more fully honored, and Christ more faithfully obeyed. But in every instance I have returned from the examination of the infallible Word with increased confidence in the general scripturalness of our doctrine and polity. As I understand the teachings of our Lord and his inspired Apostles, I cannot honestly be otherwise than what I have been from the beginning; and though I should, for all reasons, prefer the name which was given to believers at Antioch, and am always grieved when I think of the multiplicity of names by which that comprehensive and appropriate designation has been overlaid and degraded; yet, as circumstances are, — as the Christian host is divided and subdivided into a great variety of sects, every one with its distinctive appellation, — I am not ashamed of the one by which we are recognized. It is not wanting in antiquity, and, as now understood, it is sufficiently expressive. It denotes what I really am, and what you are, and what, without a new revelation, we expect to be until we shall join that portion of "the whole family" to every one of whom is given "a new name which no man knoweth, saving he that receiveth it." Nor am I, by comparison, ashamed of my company; for, although there may be some persons and some things among us that I suppose could well be spared, and others that might be greatly improved, yet here are a people with whom I can happily lábor for Christian ends, and from whom I should count it an affliction to be separated. To the practical development of those principles which we have learned at the feet of our great Teacher, my life is devoted. Whatever, therefore, you may find in this fraternal communication, you need not be reluctant to receive on the ground of any apprehension that the writer has changed his views, or is becoming indifferent to the claims of any truth or any duty. "I can do nothing against the truth;" my heart's desire is to do something "for the truth."

Now, dear brother, before we proceed to another sentence, let us bow our "knees unto the God and Father of our Lord Jesus Christ, of whom the whole family in heaven and earth is named," imploring the illuminations of that Divine Spirit, in whose "light we see light," and by whose gracious influence we are ever prepared to receive, as well as qualified to discover, the truth. Were a form needed, we have one sufficiently appropriate in the "Collect for Unity."

"O God, the Father of our Lord Jesus Christ, our only Saviour, the Prince of Peace, give us grace seriously to lay to heart the great dangers we are in by our unhappy divisions. Take away all hatred and prejudice, and whatsoever else may hinder us from godly union and concord; that, as there is but one Body, and one Spirit, and one Hope of our calling, one Lord, one Faith, one Baptism, one God and Father of us all, so we may henceforth be all of one heart, and of one soul, united in one holy bond of truth and peace, of faith and charity, and may with one mind and one mouth glorify Thee, through Jesus Christ our Lord. Amen."

I take it for granted that every one, who would make good his title to the name of CHRISTIAN, will agree with me that the interest which seems to be awakened with respect to the great question of Christian union, is a very encouraging feature of our most interesting age. Whatever may be thought of the many treatises upon the subject with which our heads and hearts are so faithfully plied; or, whatever our estimate of the diversified theories which are proposed, indicating modes by which it is confidently insisted that the desirable end can be attained, we must all feel and acknowledge that the very idea of harmonious concert among Christians of every name is creditable to the period in which it is cordially entertained; and that the extent to which this idea, so full of promise to the Church[1] and the world, is countenanced and cherished by the present generation of believers, concurs with other facts to distinguish the nineteenth century from a long series of its predecessors. I concede that in every period since the first schism in the Church of Christ, there have been good men of various communions who have deplored the evils of division, and lifted up a voice of strength in earnest rebuke of the spirit of sectarianism, and fervently implored the great Founder to re-melt, and re-unite, and re-mould the alienated fragments. But, in our day, this interest is not confined to a few; it is felt, deeply and solemnly, by the great majority of the truly spiritual, the working class of every evangelical denomination.

The causes which have contributed especially to awaken such attention to this important subject, may doubtless be found in certain great facts which happily distinguish our times from all that have preceded them since the martyrdom of the Apostles; — such as the enlarged effusion of the Holy Spirit, who is preëminently the "Repairer of the breach, the Restorer of paths to dwell in;" the prevalence of religious revivals,

[1] I shall often use the term Church in its broad acceptation, as denoting the whole body of professed believers, irrespective of their distinctive names.

which are always, so far as they are genuine, conducive to Christian affection and concord; the efforts of all evangelical denominations to convert the heathen to Christ — a service in which they practically ascertain the importance of agreement and coöperation; and the increased acquaintance of different sects with one another, resulting from their frequent assemblage and familiar intercourse in voluntary associations, where they have learned to hold in courteous abeyance their distinctive peculiarities, and, taking their high position, side by side, on the broad maximum of agreement, to be fraternal co-workers in a common enterprise. The practical tendencies of the age have given to the question a practical form; and, while thousands have concurred in both feeling and opinion that something ought to be done to restore union, — that union which the Saviour commanded, and for which he prayed, — the general inquiry has been, and still is, what? What should be done? What can be done? The object is good; is it attainable? Much has been said and much written, — not all, perhaps, the wisest, or the best adapted to accomplish the cherished purpose, — yet, all indicative of a painful conviction that somewhere there is flagrant wrong, and that it is high time the wrong should be sought out, and, like the dross that hinders fused metal from welding, be put forever away.

It is no part of my design to examine the theories which have been advanced upon this subject, or to propose any specific plan of my own for the reünion of the dismembered body of Christ. My object is rather to explain what I suppose to be the union at which all Christians should aim; to point out some of the evil effects of disunion; to suggest reasons why we should do all we can, consistently with faithful allegiance to Christ, to promote the union of all his disciples; and to indicate methods by which we may aid in the production of so important a result. I shall not intermeddle with the cherished principles or the polity of any denomination of Christians, but shall endeavor to confine myself to matters which are extraneous to whatever any sect may regard as fundamental to its own ecclesiastical organization. My present concern is more with the *spirit* of sect, than with its constitution, or creed, or discipline.

And may the Holy Spirit, "from whom all holy desires, all good counsels, and all just works do proceed," so inspire and direct as that there shall be no violation of that great melting, combining principle, the charity which "rejoiceth in the truth," and is "the bond of perfectness."

I.

THE UNION THAT IS DESIRABLE.

THE Saviour required his disciples to be united, and for their oneness he prayed. Can there be any diversity of opinion as to the extent of his meaning, when he said, "One is your Master, even Christ, and ALL YE are brethren?" Or, when he said, "Other sheep I have which are not of this fold; them also I must bring, and they shall hear my voice; and there shall be ONE FOLD, and one shepherd?" Or, when he said, "A new commandment I give unto you, that ye love one another," and enforced the requirement by proposing his own example as the model for our imitation, — "As I have loved you, that ye also love one another?" Or, when he prayed with touching earnestness, "That they may be one, even as we are; I in thee, and thou in me, that they may be made PERFECT IN ONE: neither pray I for these alone, but for them also who shall believe on me through their word; that they ALL may be one, as thou, Father, art in me, and I in thee, that they also may be ONE IN US?" The idea of union which dwelt in his mind, while uttering such language, is unquestionably the idea which ought to exist, unmodified, in our minds, and in accordance with which we should faithfully shape our whole spirit and conduct. The Saviour foresaw and appreciated the mischiefs that would result from the divisions and alienations and strifes of his professed followers; and he as perfectly understood the benefits which would accrue, both to themselves and to a perishing world, provided they would affectionately coöperate in their Master's service. Hence the frequency and the earnestness with which he referred to this point, and the diversified methods which he adopted to impress upon his people the importance of remaining undivided.

The kind of union that is to be desired and sought, may be seen in the primitive Churches, not, indeed, in absolute perfection, but in the best form that has ever been exhibited. After the number of disciples had greatly increased, so as to be counted by thousands, it is testified of them, and much to their credit, as well as to the honor of Christianity, that "The whole multitude of them that believed were of ONE HEART, and ONE SOUL." No one doubts that they kept "the unity of the spirit in the bond of peace;" that they had "one Lord, one Faith, one Baptism;" that they were to a degree never since surpassed, united, and that they realized in large measure the blessedness of those who feel and act as "ONE in Christ Jesus," for "they were all filled with the Holy Ghost, and spake the word of God with great boldness," and "great grace was upon them all," and "the Lord added to the church daily the saved."[1] Assuredly, the Church was then one, presenting to the world the image of a happy, united family; all the children of one Father; all the disciples of one Teacher; "all by one Spirit baptized into one body;" all "partakers of one bread;" all actuated by one desire, and moving in one line toward one grand result. According to the prediction, they had "one heart and one way;" they "served the Lord with one consent;" they were often "with one accord in one place;" they had access through "one Mediator," by "one Spirit," to "one God and Father of all;" they were joint-heirs to one inheritance;

> "Their fears, their hopes, their aims were one,
> Their comforts and their cares."

When shall the Redeemer again behold upon the earth a scene so resplendent with moral beauty? When shall a selfish world again yield before the moral energy of such Christians?

This delightful union was maintained for a con-

[1] Τοὺς σωζομένους.

siderable period without essential change. Questions of expediency and policy occasionally arose that threatened to interrupt the harmony of feeling; but how soon and how happily were all discordant views adjusted the moment they were submitted to the intelligent and peace-loving, peace-making, Apostles! Converts from all nations were introduced in large numbers; and yet, notwithstanding the wide diversities in their intellectual character, their early training, their systems of philosophy, their modes of worship, they were so effectually assimilated by the renewing Spirit, that they blended most harmoniously into one body, and were no longer Jew or Samaritan, Greek or Barbarian, Platonist or Epicurean, Pharisee or Sadducee, Circumcised or Uncircumcised, but were all "one in Christ," and their one name was CHRISTIAN. Naturally enough, the converts were particularly attached to the ministers by whom they believed, and in a few instances, as at Corinth, this personal preference for "*my* minister" assumed an objectionable form, and called for pointed reprehension; but many years passed before this or any other evil effectuated those radical divisions which have since occasioned so injurious a disruption of the ligaments of Christian fellowship. With the exception of some minor dissensions that were only temporary and easily healed, and an occasional outbreak of party spirit or selfish rivalry that a single reproof would quell, — all indicative that the Church in her holiest period was imperfect, — the Christianity of the first century was distinguished by a degree of union among her disciples that no subsequent age has witnessed. No divisions affected their real unity, or prevented their affectionate coöperation in the great enterprise which their Master had charged them to execute. Hence, the intelligent Waddington, when speaking of the early Christians, justly says that "their variations were without schism, and their differences without acrimony."

From the recorded Acts of the Apostles, as well as from their Epistles, we learn how pacific was their spirit, and how studiously they sought to preserve inviolate the unity and the fellowship of all the followers of Christ. Let any person read these portions of the inspired volume, with candid and careful reference to the point now under consideration, and he will be not only surprised at the amount of attention which the Apostles bestowed upon it, but deeply impressed with the importance which they manifestly attached to it. To such a reader it will be clearly obvious that the idea of Christian union, of which I have spoken as dwelling in the mind of their incarnate Lord, had been, by some process, transferred entire to their minds, and that they were earnestly desirous to transfer it, unmodified, to the minds of all believers, Jew and Gentile. Everywhere do we find them teaching that Christians, irrespective of national, civil, social distinctions, are incorporated into one society, and that Christ is the basis and the bond of this association; "for he is our peace," said they, "who hath made both one, and hath broken down the middle wall of partition between us . . . . to make in himself of twain one new man, so making peace." Well has it been said that "this two fold doctrine is a subject which imparts an entire character to some of the epistles, and which furnishes a clew to much in nearly all." Any reader, by taking this clew, may ascertain for himself the character of the apostolic spirit and the bearings of apostolic influence; and, if he has any acquaintance with the power of religious teachers, by one course to promote Christian harmony, or by an opposite course to foment unchristian discord, he will not wonder, after a careful study of the writings, the labors, and the spirit of the Apostles, that during their lives the Church was essentially one harmonious and devoted brotherhood. And if he is one who truly grieves over the separations, and contentions, and dishonors of God's people, he will mournfully exclaim, "O that none but men of such principles and such tempers had ever been found among their guides and teachers!" Alas! how soon was the true apostolic succession interrupted, and men of selfish motives and belligerent dispositions allowed to disjoint and scatter, in mangled fragments, the body which Paul and Peter, John and James, left compactly and beautifully one! The Lord in mercy give to his Churches once more a ministry whose influence shall be soothing, healing, nourishing!

The desirable union among the friends of Christ is precisely that which we find so clearly sketched and made illustriously prominent in the New Testament. It is that which the Saviour so tenderly and impressively enjoined upon his followers, and for the completeness and universality and perpetuity of which he, on his way to the Garden of Sorrows, and in anticipation of the cross, so fervently prayed. It is that which is so delightfully represented as having existed in "the multitude of them that believed" at Jerusalem, — that nucleus of the Church universal, — the very model in faith, and love, and obedience, to which all ecclesiastical organizations should have been faithfully conformed. It is that which the Apostles and their coädjutors in the sacred ministry sought most studiously to maintain around the cross as the central attraction and the bond of fellowship, and which they were successful, to a wonderful extent, in preserving unbroken till the last of them went up to receive his reward. Let all Christians be like their primitive brethren, believing what they believed, loving as they loved, obeying as they obeyed, and the union of the first century will be the union of the nineteenth century.

You, my brother, will regard me as sufficiently specific and definite. By descending to particulars, I should be liable to an assumption of the prerogatives of an interpreter, and thus meddle with a department that is foreign to my plan, and subversive of my main design. And yet, I hesitate not to say that, while I thus speak in general terms of the union which the New Testament recommends and illustrates by examples, as the kind of union that is desirable, I have no difficulty in determining for myself what the New Testament teaches upon this subject. Is it in any sense doubtful what the Saviour required his disciples to be and to do, that they might be united to him and to one another? Does any obscurity rest upon the inspired record of the belief, the spirit, or the practice, of the primitive Churches? Are the Apostles at all equivocal in their teachings with respect to the kind of agreement and assimilation that is essential to real, permanent union? Is there any reason to suppose, that among the Christians of the first century, there were various sects, and that their union consisted in affectionate association irrespective of diversity of sentiment and practice? Does any one believe that the early Churches had different and clashing creeds, or that they administered the ordinances in various and dissimilar forms?

The waters that encompass the globe are known by different names, as the Atlantic, the Pacific, the Baltic, the Mediterranean; but these names denote only territorial distinctions, never suggesting the idea of difference of quality. They commingle and coälesce without any indications of either chemical or mechanical disfellowship.[1] So also in the age of the Apostles there were territorial divisions among Christians, for there were the "Churches in Judea," the "Churches in Asia," the "Churches in Macedonia," and in many other countries and provinces; but these names never denoted any diversity in creed, spirit, or form. Christians of every country, every color, every condition, were spiritually, doctrinally, practically one. Such is the oneness now desirable;

1 "Circumquaque porro infatigati fertur fluctus oceani; unus quidem, sed multis cognominibus instructus." — *Dion.*

and happy will be that day when we can speak of the Churches in England, Burmah, Denmark, Jamaica, Virginia, Illinois, Rhode Island, Nova Scotia, and, knowing no other distinction than the geographical, can recognize all these companies of believers as one; so that when their members pass from one country or one State to another, they may everywhere be welcomed, not as belonging to a particular denomination, but as belonging to Christ, and following in "the footsteps of the flock."[1] Party names must be dropped, party lines must be obliterated, party spirit must be put away, party measures must be discontinued; and all Christians must have "one heart and one way;" then will there be the desirable union, — that which the Son of God requires of his people as essential to the full development of their character, and to their largest usefulness as his representatives and witnesses.

[1] "The union of Christians on earth is perfectly consistent with many churches, each complete in itself. There is no visible centre of unity on earth to the Christian Church, as there was to the Jewish. In the Jewish Church, one candlestick with its seven branches typified the Church of God in complete unity, as confined to one nation, with one central place of union at Jerusalem; but in the Gentile churches the emblem is different. There are seven golden candlesticks, and in the midst of them one like unto the Son of man." — *Bickersteth.*

II.

CONSIDERATIONS THAT RENDER CHRISTIAN UNION DESIRABLE.

These, my dear brother, cannot be adequately represented without a more particular and extended reference, than I could wish were necessary, to the deplorable mischiefs of division. It would be far more agreeable to confine my observation, and solicit your attention, to the more illuminated and cheering side of the picture, — to that delightful state of things which we anticipate, not in our day, but somewhere in the brightening future, when shall return the palmy scenes of primitive unanimity, primitive affection, and primitive concert; when "Ephraim shall not envy Judah, and Judah shall not vex Ephraim;" when party names shall all be merged and disappear in the one sufficient designation, Christian; when "there shall be one fold," as well as "one Shepherd;" when the whole sacramental host of God shall rally around one standard, the blood-red Cross, all prompt to obey the orders of one Leader, all submissively and peacefully "following the Lamb whithersoever he goeth." How inspiring, how soul-elevating the anticipation! Lovely as was the landscape to the natural eye when the "dew descended upon the mountains of Zion," imparting freshness to vegetation, far lovelier to the moral vision will be that scene of moral beauty where "BRETHREN DWELL TOGETHER IN UNITY," and in view of which all holy beings will exclaim, "Behold, how good and how pleasant!" That is a scene which, with pencil dipped in the "rainbow round about the throne," I would fain describe. But, alas! it is one which has never greeted my eye, nor has it greeted yours. Our predecessors through long ages, and many of our cotemporaries, have desired to see it,

"But died without the sight."

It is a state of things which we contemplate only by the visual power of faith. Inspired history has sketched it on the Past, when the Church was young, elastic, and fair, with a single Head to control her movements, and a single Heart to send the common element of life to her extremities. Imagination gives vividness to the picture; we admire it as the ideal of moral loveliness; and yet we admire with a sigh that it finds no actual counterpart in the Present. Inspired prophecy has painted it on the Future, and shown us the

Church in the vigor of meridian life, one and indivisible, well-proportioned and athletic, radiant with glory, — "fair as the moon, clear as the sun, and terrible as an army with banners." And here, as we gaze, our hearts are fired with rapture, and naught interposes to diminish the "joy of hope," but the saddening reflection that the scene we are viewing still lies in the dim perspective, and that earth may roll off many more of its probationary years before it will be hailed as a present reality, and we cry, "O Lord, how long?"

But while the blessed effects of genuine Christian Brotherhood belong to a department of observation where we walk by faith, the evils of schism are present and come within the realizations of sight. And so long as these evils exist, — and exist they will till schism is no more, — we gain nothing valuable by refusing to consider them, or to open our minds to a full conviction of their perniciousness. I may probaby be told that some good has accrued to the Church and to the world, from the distribution of Christians into separate and rival sects, and that in strict justice I ought to mention the benefits as well as the injuries of division. Benefits of Christian disunion! And is the brother who makes this intimation, really in earnest? Were I treating of the Divine dispensations towards the grievously imperfect, I might show how God has manifested "the riches of his goodness, and forbearance, and long-suffering," by patiently enduring "their manners in the wilderness," and proved himself wise and able to educe some good from so great a mass of heaven-hated enormity. But, surely, it will not be pretended that the benefits referred to counterbalance one in a thousand of the known and felt evils; or that they are really more than incidental effects secured by the wisdom and power of an over-ruling Providence; or that they constitute, all together, any valid reason why schism should be continued another day. I may, then, without the imputation of injustice or one-sidedness, pass them over, as not properly belonging to my subject; at the same time rendering gratitude to God that he has applied his infinite faculties to the eduction of good from a source so fearfully charged with pernicious elements; that he has so counteracted the tendencies to decomposition as to preserve life in the divided membership; and that he has, in any degree, caused a system of wrong that, like all sin, is infernal in its origin, and destructive in its bearings, to glorify his holy Name.

As it is neither important to my object, nor consistent with the brevity which I wish to study, that I should attempt a minute and extended description of all the evils of disunion among Christians, I shall limit my specifications to a few of the more prominent; and these I mention for the sole purpose of exhibiting more fairly and forcibly the reasons why we should seek a restoration of that harmony which we all concur in regarding as desirable.

1. THE INJURIOUS EFFECT OF DIVISION UPON THE PIETY OF THE CHURCH.

The Church consists of individuals, every one of whom is a distinct being, possessing capabilities all his own, and directly responsible for his character and conduct to his final Judge. The piety of the Church, therefore, is neither more nor less than the sum of the piety of all her members; just as her numerical strength is the sum of all the persons included in her membership. And there is no way of improving or deteriorating her piety but by improving or deteriorating the piety of her individual constituents. Whatever, therefore, has an unfavorable effect upon the personal holiness of her members, is detrimental to the holiness of the body.

The Gospel recognizes us all as moral beings in the process of training for a higher position, and requires that, by availing ourselves of the abundant provisions of the new covenant, we should individually aim at the formation of perfect religious character. We are not authorized to be satisfied with anything less than complete conformity to all the laws under which God our Moral Governor has placed us. To the production of such a result, all the agencies and instrumentalities of the system of Grace are wisely adapted; and it is not only recommended as a privilege, but commanded as a duty, and encouraged by promises, that, in the use of appointed means, we should "grow in grace," and "go on unto perfection." "Be ye holy," is the unrepealable requirement. Christ, the atoning Saviour, "gave himself for us, that he might redeem us from all iniquity," freely pouring out his blood which "cleanseth us from all sin." The truths which he communicated, and the duties which he enjoined, and the discipline which he appointed, and the hopes which he encouraged, all have reference to this end, the complete sanctification of his people. When he "ascended up far above all heavens," he "gave gifts unto men," such as apostles, evangelists, prophets, pastors, and teachers, all "for the perfecting of the saints, for the work of the ministry, for the edifying of the body of Christ, till we all come in the unity of the spirit, and of the knowledge of the Son of God, unto a perfect man, unto the measure of the stature of the fulness of Christ." The Apostle Paul assures us that the object he had in view, while "warning every man, and teaching every man, in all wisdom," was that he "might present every man perfect in Christ Jesus." "This also we wish," he says, "even your perfection;" and his prayer for his brethren was, that the God of Peace—not the God of dissension, but "the very God of Peace"—would "sanctify you wholly, and preserve your whole body, and soul, and spirit, blameless unto the coming of our Lord Jesus Christ."

Whatever may be the opinions of Christians as to the practicability of certain attainments in the present life, I suppose it is the desire of every one to be "cleansed from all unrighteousness," and the prayer of every one that God would "create" in him "a clean heart," and the habit of every one to "press toward the mark for the prize," "perfecting holiness in the fear of God." And I presume that every Christian, in his pursuit of that "holiness, without which no man shall see the Lord," has found his soul entangled by influences that interfere with his progress,—influences from which he is obliged to disengage himself before he can successfully proceed. Incumbered with weights, how could the racer outstrip his competitors? Ensnared by besetting sins, or by anything that compresses or restrains the free-born spirit, how can the Christian bound onward as he should in the highway of the redeemed, the "way of holiness" that is cast up for the convenience of the Lord's ransomed?

Have you, my brother, never perceived the injurious tendency, in this respect, of the sectarian divisions among the professed followers of Christ? Is not the spirit of sect enthralling in its influence—preventing, like a tether, the ascent of the soul into that fulness of freedom for which it longs and sighs? And just in proportion as a soul has been emancipated from that spirit, allowing its affections to spread out over the whole multitude of the redeemed, has it not felt itself unbound, and facilitated in its soarings into a region where its atmosphere is purer, and its horizon wider?

It was the prayer of an ancient Christian, eminent for his struggles after personal holiness:

> "Coarctationes cordis mei dilata;
> Et ex angustiis meis educ me."

He perceived, he felt the evils of a contracted heart, and desired its dilatation. Confined within narrow limits, he could neither breathe freely, nor work effectively, and he prayed to be led out into a larger place. Said another, whose piety was of still higher order: "I will run in the way of thy commandments, when thou shalt enlarge my heart." And the Apostle Paul exhorted the members of a certain Church whom he desired to be eminently holy: "Be ye also enlarged."

The injurious bearing of this great evil, in one direction at least, is very justly described by a powerful writer of our own country. "Upon the *religious intellect*," says the late Rev. Dr. Mason, "sectarian feelings and fellowship produce an effect analogous to that of the division of labor upon mechanical ingenuity. By concentrating its operations in a few points, or perhaps in a single one, they render it peculiarly acute and discriminating within those limits, at the expense of enfeebling or destroying its general power. Conversations are cherished, books are read, time expended, faculties employed, not for the purpose of acquiring larger views of the Redeemer's truth, grace, kingdom and glory; but for the purpose of training more accurate disputants upon the heads of sectarian collision. Here men distinguish themselves; here they shine; here they gratify their vanity, which they often mistake for conscience."

Perhaps I cannot do better than to quote the same writer's remarks touching the influence of this spirit upon the *practical judgment.* "This," he says, "is clearly seen in the estimate which animated sectarians form of character. The good qualities of their own adherent they readily perceive, admire, and extol; his failings they endure with patience; and his faults, which they dare not justify, they can overlook and extenuate. But, should he quit their connection, the first are disparaged, the second are no longer tolerable, and the third swell into crimes. On the other hand, virtues and graces in a different party, they are apt to admit with reluctance, and rarely without qualification. But, lo! all is altered! . . . . Our breasts fill with the milk of human kindness; and we welcome to our hearts the very man whom, a week before, we eyed askance, and should have thought to have been a spot in our feast of charity. Nay, we are often summarily convinced that a person of dubious character has been injured and persecuted. Our inquiries are conducted with the nicest delicacy. So gentle our temper! so charitable our construction! so large an allowance for infirmity! so deep our sympathy! Whence the miracle? Has a seraph, with fire from the altar of God, touched these men of unclean lips, and taken away the stains which alarmed our purity?

Oh no! They are precisely what they were. Wherefore, then, this change in eyesight, in feelings, in behaviour? Simple inquirer, thou knowest nothing of party magic! They have come, or are coming, or are expected to come, over to us."

If such are vicious tendencies of the spirit of sect, — and who will venture the averment that they are not? — then it is not difficult to see how the *heart* may be injuriously affected, and the quality of one's religion seriously impaired. If the religious intellect is thus dwarfed and shrivelled down to the diminutiveness of an inferior particular which it habitually contemplates and elaborates; and if the practical judgment is thus perverted and seduced into wrong estimates of the good and evil of moral character, just according as that character is identified with *our* party, or *their* party; surely the moral feelings will not remain uncontracted, unperverted, unseduced, but will inevitably suffer a deplorable deterioration. It is an office of religion to enlarge and ennoble the little mind, by making it familiar with great subjects, filling it with great ideas, prompting it to the accomplishment of great ends, opening upon its observation great scenes, giving it a great field for the free play of its faculties and affections, proposing a great Model for imitation, holding out a great prize as the reward of great endeavors. The sectarian spirit reduces the great mind — it would the mind of an angel — to narrow dimensions, by restricting its contemplations, its solicitudes, its aims, its efforts to insignificant matters, often microscopic points, unbefitting the dignity of its nature and the glory of its destiny.

Another damaging effect of the divisions among Christians is, that, whatever the sect in which we choose our home, we are likely to find the field of our *affections* circumscribed. Few will acknowledge the truth of this statement until they shall have examined facts and analyzed their own feelings. Accustomed to compression, we may be unaware of the stringencies of our condition, and think ourselves free when we are unduly restrained. Those who are without the limits of our particular denomination, provided we think on the whole that they are Christians, we may regard with some favor, and we may say some kind words respecting them, and sigh out some occasional regrets that such good people should not be altogether such as we are. The feeling which we cherish towards them we denominate by the sacred name of Charity, — a term which has been robbed of its true import, just in proportion as the godlike quality which it denotes has been transmuted into something spurious. In the days and in the writings of the Apostles it represented the crowning excellence, the uppermost stratum of the pyramid of graces, of which faith was the lowest, resting on "the Rock of salvation." Charity was then Love, and nothing else; and, apart from it, as the finish and adornment, religious character was a deformity. But in our times, the word has become the name of a mingled feeling, in which good-will, condescension, and even pity, are the ingredients measured out with all the nicety and cautiousness of a medical prescription. Charity! Yes, Charity, in the modern acceptation of the term, is that which we give to Christians who "follow not with us." "On the whole, notwithstanding their defects, I have charity for them," is the very significant admission which Christ daily hears from the lips of his redeemed, renewed, dependent disciples! "I love them, notwithstanding some deficiencies," would convey to any hearer a different idea. But "brotherly love" is too often reserved for the party to which the individual belongs,—yes, that is the word, *belongs;* for a party-man in religion is not his own, nor is he Christ's,—he belongs to his party. It is natural—and the propriety of the feeling, within certain limits, need not be questioned—that we should feel a special regard for those Christians whose principles and spirit and conduct we consider as most completely scriptural; but even here there is peculiar danger lest we should prefer them because they coincide with ourselves, rather than because they most nearly resemble the Saviour, and have the largest measure of his approbation. Do we take them to our hearts because of their attainments in the higher Christian life, or because of their exact conformity to our opinions and practices? You are not ignorant, my brother, that such is the power of the selfishness which is nurtured by sectarian divisions as to render it easier to regard with special favor a man of moderate piety in one's own denomination, than a man of uncommon holiness who stands associated with a Christian people of another name.

How difficult, under such circumstances, must be the formation of a complete religious character! How difficult, when the benevolent feelings are thus restricted, to be "made perfect in love!" How much real excellence is there in loving those who love us, and who love us for the same reasons that we love them? Well did Jesus inquire, "Do not even the publicans the same?" No increase of such love can properly be called growth in grace.

It is a peculiarity of the recent convert that he loves all who exhibit the spirit and maintain the life of the Christian; and when he thinks of avowing publicly his attachment to the Saviour, and connecting himself by covenant with the people of God, it is inexpressibly painful that he cannot follow his convictions of duty without identifying himself with a sect, and thus inclosing himself within walls which he shall be pledged to strengthen and defend, — walls of separation, of which he reads nothing in his Bible, — walls which divide believers not so much from the world as from other believers. Thousands in our Churches remember well the simplicity and tenderness of their feelings at the time of their spiritual infancy, and the process by which those feelings were schooled into submission to what they learned to regard as unavoidable necessity. With aching hearts they inquired, "Why are Christians thus broken into separate and rival sects? Why are they not, as I read they were in apostolic times, all one?" And they ceased not to ask such questions until the Christian feeling had declined, and the sectarian feeling had gained the ascendency. And, occasionally, at subsequent periods, as their piety has been revived and the work of grace has been deepened in their souls, have these questions recurred only to remain unanswered as before; while the feeling that prompted them, has, by a similar process, been gradually smothered and silenced. On this subject I deal not in conjectures; I speak what I know, and testify that which I have seen. Every Christian is convinced that to unite with a sect is better than to make no profession of religion; but there are multitudes, of more than one denomination, who regard the alternative as a choice of evils, the whole of which they would gladly avoid. They painfully feel the power of the temptations to which, by a sectarian profession, they are inevitably exposed,— temptations which they cannot successfully resist, except by withdrawing or greatly weakening their vigilance at other points which need their guardian forces. The position which they have assumed, the influences by which they are encompassed, and, above all, the subtle power of diabolical agency, render it extremely difficult for them to keep their affections flowing forth, as they would have them, over all barriers, and encircling in their comprehensive embrace the entire "household of faith." In such circumstances, the cultivation of brotherly love, such as the New Testament both requires and illustrates, is a task of no ordinary magnitude, and the wonder is not, that there is so little of this large-hearted affection among Christians of differing sects, but that, in our divided and alienated condition, there is any. So far as we possess this element of Christian character, let us be grateful, and own that by the grace of God we are, in this particular, what we are. And let us henceforth be doubly vigilant, lest our consciences should be ensnared by the vicious delusion that love of sect is, under our peculiar circumstances, all that our Master requires; and lest we should illegitimately infer that the more we have of this narrowed "love to the brethren," the stronger may be our assurance that "we have passed from death unto life." Who are "the brethren?" Are not all who have received "the adoption of sons," and been made "partakers of the Divine nature," and have one Father by their new creation in Christ Jesus? Are not all who "draw near to God" through the same Mediator and by the same Divine agency? Are not all whom God has "accepted in the Beloved," justifying them by that "righteousness which is unto all and upon all them that believe," and shedding abroad his love in their hearts by the Holy Ghost? Are not all who have "good hope through grace" warming their bosoms, and not only animating them under all the troubles and conflicts of this life, but promising to do so amidst the languors and agonies of their last moments? Disobedient they may be in some things which we think important, and yet they are believers in Christ; they are "fellow-citizens of the saints;" their names are in the Book of Life; they are heirs to the heavenly inheritance. If we love them not as brethren, and "heirs together with us," how can we say that we have fellowship with God? How say that we love the invisible Father, when we love not his visible children,—his "whole family?"

The unfavorable influence of our sectarian divisions is manifest also in their effect upon our study of the Sacred Volume. It is not an unusual complaint among ministers, that they find it extremely difficult to read the Bible for devotional purposes without frequent distraction of mind, and diversion of thought and feeling from their proper object. Passages strike their attention as affording topics for sermons, or choice proof-texts in support of some favorite theory, and their intellects work in that direction, while their hearts remain unimpressed, unrefreshed; and they bend the knee in prayer with no benefit from the warming, quickening Word. Similar is the tendency of our minds, when habituated to sectarian reflections and discussions, to wander from the true objects of Biblical investigation, and to regard that precious treasury of truth as merely an armory from which may be drawn the weapons of our warfare, not with God's enemies, not with our own enemies, but with brethren who do not coincide with us in all points of systematic divinity, or all the formularies of Christian worship, or all the triangularities of ecclesiastical organization.

Among the primary objects with reference to which we should "search the Scriptures," one is, that we may obtain the food requisite to the nourishing of the life of God in our own souls. The Bible is the storehouse of spiritual nutriment, containing "the sincere milk of the word" for the infantile and feeble, and the "strong meat" suited to them who are of "full age." It was the testimony of Moses, in advanced life, and as the result of a long experience, and his statement was corroborated by the Saviour, that "Man doth not live by bread only, but by every word that proceedeth out of the mouth of the Lord." "Thy words were found," said a prophet, "and I did eat them;" and Job declared that he esteemed the words of God's mouth more than his necessary food. Every spiritual Christian knows that he advances in the divine life, and has his graces developed and strengthened, only so far as he receives and inwardly digests the nutritious truths which his provident Father has garnered up for his family in the Old and New Testaments. Having opened to him such a copiousness of good things, which he has often found to be sweet to his taste and invigorating to his whole spiritual constitution, he wonders not at the Divine requirement, " Grow in grace, and in the knowledge of our Lord Jesus Christ," and he is not surprised to find that they who live by faith upon God's word are spiritually " fat and flourishing," and strong in soul for Christian labor. Why should it not be so, when they are fed with " the finest of the wheat," and " satisfied with honey out of the Rock," and refreshed daily with " water out of the wells of salvation ?" Seest thou a professor of Christianity spiritually lean, gaunt, haggard—know assuredly that he lives not upon the " children's bread."

Another object should be that we may ascertain the duties which God would have us perform. Before the revealed Word was furnished, the inquirer for the Divine will resorted directly to God, and asked for specific directions. But, since the completion of the Sacred Volume, and the discontinuance of Inspiration, the inquiries of Christians, not only as to what they shall believe, but also as to what they shall practise, are directed to these heavenly oracles. He who studies the Bible with a sincere desire to learn his duties, and with a full determination to perform them, never fails of success; for the Saviour declares that " if any man will do," "he shall know;" and that if any man will follow him, "he shall not walk in darkness, but shall have the light of life." Such a Christian will gratefully confess to God: "Thy word is a lamp unto my feet, and a light unto my path." It is indeed the "more sure" source of practical illumination "unto which we do well that we take heed as unto a light that shineth in a dark place till the day dawn," and we find ourselves in a land where "there is no night." Blessed Book! all "given by inspiration of God, and profitable for doctrine, for reproof, for correction, for instruction in righteousness; that the man of God may be perfect, thoroughly furnished unto ALL GOOD WORKS."

A third object is, that we may become familiar with the truths by which we are to advance the spiritual benefit of our fellow-men. Christians are appointed to an important agency in promoting the salvation of men. The instrumentality which they are required to employ, and to which the Holy Spirit gives efficiency, is the Divine Word. The truths of the Bible are the arrows, "sharp in the heart of the King's enemies," that do execution. Jesus, after declaring important truths, added, "These things I say that ye might be saved;" and his petition for his chosen, was, "Sanctify them through thy truth; thy word is truth;" and he assured them, "Now ye are clean [καθαρόι] through the word which I have spoken unto you." The Apostles regarded the Gospel — that glorious system of truth addressed to free agents — as the grand instrumentality by which they were to destroy sin and build up holiness in the world; and with that instrumentality they made themselves carefully and extensively acquainted, that so, being "mighty in the Scriptures," they could "with great power" execute their mission of mercy. The truths of the Bible are "the weapons of our warfare," "mighty through God" to the demolition of Satan's "strongholds" in human hearts, human philosophies, and human customs; and they are also the implements of wondrous efficacy by which we prepare the materials, and build upon the one Foundation of that spiritual edifice which consists of "lively stones," "fitly framed together," and which "groweth unto a holy temple in the Lord." He, therefore, — whether he be a "master-builder" or a "worker together with him," — who would show himself "a workman approved unto God, that needeth not to be ashamed, rightly dividing the word of truth," must make himself familiarly acquainted with that "word of truth." Let his soul be deeply impregnated with the spirit of his Master; and then, with the Bible in his heart, and in his hand, and upon his tongue, — the Bible understood, loved, and skilfully used, — he will be "thoroughly furnished" as an agent of good to the Church and the world.

Such are the primary objects that the Christian should have in view as he bends his faculties to the study of God's revealed truth. With the accomplishment of such objects the sectarian spirit most injuriously interferes. It may prompt to the investigation of the Divine Oracles, and lead to the acquisition of some truth; but its object is widely diverse from those which I have specified, and from every object which a spirit inhaled at the foot of the cross would propose to accomplish. It is no part, or, at best, only a secondary and subordinate part, of its cherished design to employ its attainments in Biblical knowledge to promote the interests of personal holiness. The true sectarian does not study the Bible so much for spiritual nutriment as for theological argument. He aims, not so much at the extension of the kingdom of Christ, as at the strengthening and defending of denominational ramparts. He trains himself to the dextrous use of "the sword of the Spirit," not that he may win trophies to his Lord from the ranks of the enemy, but that he may be a skilful gladiator in controversies with a portion of his Father's children who utter not his shibboleth, or who, in the exercise of the right of private judgment, have chosen a name and adopted a polity of their own. He clothes himself with a panoply, not "the whole armor of God," as described by an Apostle, but one which he has manufactured more for the protection of his intellect than his heart, of his theological consistency than his spiritual integrity; and, thus equipped, he goes forth to conflict — not with "principalities and powers," the "rulers of the darkness of this world," but with brethren whom he knows, and, if asked, acknowledges, to be "fellow-citizens of the saints, and of the household of God," and heirs with him to the promised inheritance.

Alas! what multitudes of the professed followers of Jesus are better skilled in partisan warfare than in the holy art of resisting the devil, and overcoming the world, and keeping the body under! It is admitted that "he who winneth souls is wise;" but, in their estimation, he is immensely wiser who gets the mastery in argument, and prostrates — in modern phrase, uses up — an antagonist brother. Is it not a fact, a mournful fact, that a large proportion of Christians are better versed in those points respecting which denominations differ, than those in which they agree?

Surely it requires no great perspicacity to see that our divisions, by encouraging the study of the Bible with a spirit and an intent that are adverse to the cultivation of Christian love, must have the effect to deteriorate individual piety, and impair individual usefulness.

Much might be said respecting the loss which individual piety must suffer from the amount of feeling, time, and effort, that are almost inevitably given to sectarian interests and sectarian projects, rather than to the claims of personal sanctification, or the advancement of the Christian cause. The flame of patriotism is sure to be feeble and flickering in the bosom of that man who gives to party what belongs to his country. It is not easy to be a strong partisan and also a good citizen. And there is a broader range for the affections than the nation, though it be "our own, our native land." The true man regards the interests of humanity as superior to those of nationality. He is not content with loving a single nation; he loves his race, and would benefit the whole. So is it with the Christian, who always finds the spirit of sect incompatible with enlarged devotion to Zion's welfare, and full allegiance to Zion's King. What he gives of heart and endeavor to a sect, as such, is so much withheld from the claims of general brotherhood.

And it would not be difficult to show how unhappily our schisms minister nutriment to the malign dispositions, while the better qualities are left to languish in pining atrophy. In desiring the prosperity of his own denomination, the Christian is very liable to be willing that others should suffer. In describing the progress of his own principles, he is under a strong temptation to represent the principles of others as declining in public confidence. Only by special effort can he command the magnanimity required to speak justly of the excellences belonging to another sect. Unless he is extremely careful, he will magnify the alleged errors and imperfections of others, while he extenuates or conceals whatever is objectionable in his associates. A testimony advantageous to his opponents he receives at a discount, and one that is unfavorable he accepts at a premium. "Magnes mendaciorum credulitas," is an old proverb that has not yet lost its pertinency; for credulity is still the magnet of untruths; and many such magnets are to be found in every place where the sectarian spirit prevails, drawing together loose insinuations, flying rumors, and idle conjectures, and embodying them into forms disparaging to the reputation, and detrimental to the influence, of whole bodies of Christian believers.

Should it be said that these are not uniformly or necessarily the results of sectarian division, my only reply is that they are the natural, and, in numberless cases, the actual, fruit of such division; and that the tendency, in all cases, is to the production of such fruit. To retain tenaciously our own views and practices, and yet feel, speak, and act as we should towards all who differ from us, is not indeed an impossibility, but certainly is a difficult and rare attainment. If ecclesiastical history proves anything, it furnishes abundant proof that good men often find it easier to tolerate moral obliquity of conduct than nonconformity of creed or ritual.

Well may the lovers of Christian holiness, who are striving after higher attainments in the Divine life, solemnly protest against the perpetuity of an acknowledged evil that subjects them and all their fellow-disciples to such numerous, powerful, and unnecessary temptations. Why should their consciences be exposed, gratuitously, to so many snares? Why should their benevolent feelings be so restricted and pent up by enclosures, beyond which, without extraordinary effort, they cannot pass? Why may they not read their Bibles simply and exclusively as Christians who wish to be "complete in all the will of God?" Why may they not consecrate their whole time, thought, feeling, effort, to the cultivation of holiness in themselves and others? When they would labor and pray for the entire suppression of malevolent feelings, and the full development of those which are "lovely and of good report," why should they be cruelly encompassed with influences which excite and nourish the noxious elements, and depress into dwarfish and sickly insignificance their competitors, the gracious affections? Why can they not be perfectly free to give their countenance and sympathy to "the weightier matters of the law," and of the gospel also, without incurring the suspicion that they are becoming indifferent to denominational claims? My brother, you will not blame me, if I repeat, that somewhere there is flagrant wrong, which ought at once to be repented of and put away.

2. THE INJURIOUS EFFECT OF DIVISION IN PERVERTING AND WASTING THE RESOURCES OF THE CHURCH.

Commanded by her Sovereign to spread out in affectionate concert, and conquer the revolted world, and reclaim it to himself, the Church, for a season, obeyed his instructions, and gave delightful proof of her loyalty. That the results were salutary to herself, beneficial to the world, and glorious to her honored Lord, authentic history abundantly testifies. Those were days of true Christian Fraternity in Christian Activity. One Head presided over the movements of the Church, and was reverently acknowledged; one Heart beat in her bosom, and sent to every member one element of invigorating vitality. "The whole Body, fitly framed together, and compacted by that which every joint supplieth, according to the effectual working in the measure of every part," moved forward under the direction of one Will; having in view one end, the glory of Christ; governed by one rule, the Divine Word; impelled by one motive, evangelical Love. Thus moving toward one point, and in one line, the Church moved with power, and one effect was "increase of the Body unto the edifying of itself in love." Her prayers were effectual, for they were the joint supplications of those who agreed as touching the things which they desired and asked; her testimony was convincing, because it was the concurrent testimony of thousands, among whom, without a Satanic miracle, there could have been no collusion; her endeavors were effective, for to the execution of her great enterprise, her members and her resources were unreservedly consecrated. The world saw and felt and confessed that it was plied by a moral power, before which its depravities, and philosophies, and religions, were like the chaff of the summer threshing-floor. One of her number could say, that "from Jerusalem round about unto Illyricum" he had "fully preached the gospel of Christ." In less than fifty years after the ascension of her Lord, she had not only "filled Jerusalem with her doctrine," but, according to the concession of an enemy, "the world with her converts." She was a united Church, and her fraternal coöperation was an important element of her power. She neither perverted nor wasted any of her ability by devoting it to inferior purposes; much less by employing one part of it to counteract another.

The Apostles were, one after another, sent home to their reward; and their immediate successors, partaking largely of their spirit, and acting on their plans, led on the Church still "from conquering to conquer," every day gaining new victories for her King, and every evening exclaiming, "Thanks be unto God who always causeth us to triumph in Christ, and maketh manifest by us the savor of his knowledge in every place." Happy, beyond description, for the Church and the world, if that spirit had never subsided; if those successes had never been interrupted; if the same consecration to one work had been perpetuated!

Satan's policy is to divide and weaken. By diligent search he found seams in the Christian mass, and, inserting small wedges, he found ambitious men, of questionable piety, to drive them. Stealthily, slowly, the Church became divided, and began to turn her attention from the great service assigned her, to matters of internal policy, "strifes about words," "vain jangling," and other evils, against which she had been plainly and solemnly admonished. From that period, through long centuries, her men and her means became largely devoted to the aggressive and the defensive operations of the indefinite number of feeble squadrons into which she was more and more broken. At length, by the might of the secular arm, dissent was well-nigh crushed, and what was called the Church assumed a consolidated form under an earthly head, and the night of spiritual despotism was long and dreary. The Reformation of the sixteenth century was the reviving of light and life. But it was an imperfect work, and was disfigured by divisions among its leaders, and, consequently, among their followers; and Protestantism, with all its benefits, has entailed upon the Church the evils of schism, multiform, virulent, disgraceful. The Papacy has strength in her centralization, and her control of the consciences of her millions. Protestantism has strength in her principles; but it is cut up into factions, and is immensely wasted by being perversely employed in party conflict. In Spain we have an illustration of the practical influence upon power of both union and disunion. Once she was united, and history is burdened with the record of her achievements. Subsequently, she became divided into factions, which have ever since been preying upon one another, and thwarting all designs for the common good. Now, she is one of the poorest and feeblest of the nations of Europe. Were she to talk of foreign conquest, she would be the laughing-stock of the world. Similar have been the results of schism in the Protestant Body. The Church is weakened and crippled, not merely by the division and subdivision of her numerical strength, her pecuniary resources, and her moral energy, but immensely more by the perversion and waste of her ability in that guerilla warfare, Spaniard-like, which has been kept up for three centuries. "Biting and devouring one another," sects have been "consumed one of another," — consumed as to their piety, their influence, their capabilities for usefulness. The result is, that her attempts at foreign invasion are wanting in vigor, and make but a feeble impression on the domain of the prince of darkness. And this is not all. While the sects have thus been employed in party controversies, the forces of evil have been left free to perpetrate human destruction on the largest scale. Several hamlets on the side of Etna were in danger of being destroyed by streams of lava that came pouring in their direction. The inhabitants turned out to throw up embankments and dig trenches that might divert the currents, and thus leave their homes and their property unharmed. But they were of rival and disagreed hamlets; and, heedless of the common danger, they soon began to dispute about their work, and the way of doing it; and from hard words they proceeded to harder arguments, and broke their implements of labor in rough encounter. The issue was, that the river of fire, undiverted, rolled on, and overwhelmed the dwellings and the vineyards of the bruised combatants, and they mourned, too late, the folly of their feuds and bickerings.

Am I incorrect in matters of fact? Are my conclusions illegitimate? What has the Church been doing for the last fifteen centuries? And what have been the results of her impolitic and unlovely procedures? Begin with Eusebius, and read the volumes of history which have given immortality to the humiliating record of her shame; — I mean not the histories which have been written by her enemies, and designed to hold her up to the derision and scorn of posterity, — nor yet the histories prepared by violent schismatics, abounding in misrepresentation and party abuse, — but those more impartial histories which intelligent heads and honest hearts have commended to our investigation, and upon whose statements of fact, and delineations of character, and philosophical inductions, we can rely as confidently as we can trust anything human, — and what is the conclusion to which you come, — what, but the obvious one, that the moral power of the Church has, to a deplorable extent, been squandered upon unworthy and forbidden objects? Examine the books which she has produced, only a remnant of which, indeed, have descended to our times, and what are the subjects of which they treat, what the ends at which they aim, what the spirit in which they were conceived and elaborated? If we may judge from the specimens thought worthy of preservation, or confide in the testimony of the less partial historians of successive ages, what have been the aim, the temper, the character, of the sermonizing of the Church? Have her preachers, more than a small minority, been the "peace-makers" whom the Master would pronounce "blessed" as "the sons of God?" Have they not, by tens of thousands, been distinguished for their pugnacious spirit and conduct, — the bludgeon-men of party, contending for victory, not over sin and Satan, but often over brethren, wearing, like themselves, the Christian name and the Christian livery? Has not the pulpit, which was ordained to the exhibition of Christ crucified as the Healer of human woe, been made the arena of inflammatory debate, the platform of catapeltic controversy, destructive rather than conservative, more the instrument of the Furies than of the Graces?

But we need not retire into the past to ascertain the effect of disunion upon the pulpit and the literature of the Church, or the tendency of a sectarian pulpit and a sectarian literature to pervert and waste her best resources, and thus diminish her ability to accomplish her proper service. The pulpit and the religious press are not in our day, as they should be, the consecrated vehicles of light and love. With all their improvements, resulting from the revived spirit of evangelical enterprise which appears in every department of Zion, and happily promises much greater improvements, they are still too much the engines of party spirit and party measures. Preachers, and authors, and editors, still feel it incumbent on them to superintend their respective denominational interests, and vigilantly guard, at every point, the partition walls against the attacks of the heretical; and in the support of these Defenders of the Faith, saying nothing of the aggressive class whose mission is to push invasion and make breaches, an undue amount of

Christian resources is absorbed. Nor is this the whole or the worst of the evil. The misapplication of mental power, of time, of money, is surely something to be regretted. But immensely greater is the loss resulting from the spirit that is engendered, the prejudices that are strengthened, the alienations that are aggravated. Who can estimate the evils occasioned by the enfeebling of Christian graces, the deterioration of Christian character, the perplexing of sincere inquirers, the grieving of the Holy Spirit, the hardening of unbelievers, the dishonoring of the Saviour? It may be said that Christians of all parties, to be honest, must defend their own creeds and practices, and endeavor to extend as widely as possible the views which they conscientiously believe to be Scriptural. Admitting the statement as plausible, the fact remains, that, by this process, there is an amount of wasteful expenditure for which there is no plausible apology. Physical ability and moral power, that belong to Christ and to his universal cause, are devoted to party; and, therefore, as I have twice said, there is wrong somewhere that deserves reprehension. A state of things which imposes upon Christians this seeming necessity, and involves such violations of the laws of Christian economy, cannot be justified even by sectarian sophistry.

My dear brother, are not you and I and all our fellow-disciples accountable to our redeeming Lord for the manner in which we employ ourselves, our time, our treasure, our all? And when we shall stand before him, and answer for the application of our resources, will it be acceptable to him that we have devoted a third, a fifth, or even a tenth, to the maintenance of party fortifications, or the prosecution of any mere party policy? May we never forget our responsibility to our final Judge!

During the last half-century, the different sects of the evangelical have, in addition to partisan warfare, commenced and carried forward operations of a better kind, bearing a more truly Christian aspect, and contemplating results of a higher order. How much, in these apparently benevolent activities, there may be of sectarian aims, impulses, and spirit, is best known to the Searcher of hearts. But that there is much which God approves, it would be uncandid and unjust to question. It is delightful to see the friends of Christ, even in their separate and more or less sectarian organizations, going forth to the service which has been so long and so criminally neglected. By these movements, imperfect as they have been, great good has already accrued to themselves, and great blessings have descended upon thousands of the perishing, both at home and abroad. But the experiments which they have made in the various departments of Christian enterprise, have developed most strongly the evil of which I am treating. In consequence of the prevalent divisions and the seeming impossibility of union, — perhaps, in some cases, the absence of a desire for union, — every denomination has organized its own system of machinery, to the support of which the ministry and the membership feel themselves pledged, and for the efficient action of which large demands are often made upon their liberality. Thus, in the United States, as in England, there are, in the single department of Foreign Missions, a number of these separate organizations, every one complete in itself, and any one of them capable of conducting the operations of the whole. Supposing that all the Christians in North America should be united, as were the Christians of the first century, and should agree to coöperate heartily and fully in efforts to evangelize the heathen world, it is not difficult to see that one Board or Committee, with its Secretaries, Treasurer, and Clerks, could easily superintend the whole system of operations, however extended, thus sparing many valuable men for other services, and saving a large proportion of the expense now unavoidably incurred in the support of so many sets of machinery. As matters now are, every separate missionary organization is obliged to employ, for the diffusion of information and the supply of its treasury, a large number of agents, all of whom must be paid, and who travel over mainly the same ground, at great sacrifice of time, labor, and pecuniary expense. In this particular, there would, upon the supposition of union, be an economizing of resources not at all to be despised.

You have, my brother, only to look at the multiplicity of societies, strictly denominational, and yet contemplating essentially the same ends, to be convinced that our unchristian divisions are the occasion of a most unwarrantable perversion and waste of our means of usefulness. And in view of such facts, minor though they be, compared with others, you will say that schism in the Body of Christ is censurable. If it be asked, "Where lies the responsibility of all this wrong?" that is the question which I propose to my own conscience, and which you will propose to yours.

Christianity is the patron of learning; and Christians of all denominations show their convictions of its importance by providing means for the education both of their children and their ministry. But such is the influence of the spirit of sect, that every denomination has its own institutions, from the boarding school up to the University and Theological Seminary, with Boards of Trustees, pupils and patrons mainly its own, and dependent principally upon denominational feeling and liberality for their sustentation. The mischievous results of such an arrangement are a legion. Institutions are unnecessarily multiplied, and by consequence are neither endowed nor adequately supported.[1] Suitable libraries and other parts of the desirable apparatus of education are not furnished. Instructors are not so well paid as to induce them to seek the highest qualifications for their employment. An elevated order of education is not provided for; and that for which provision is made, is liable to take on a sectarian coloring and configuration. For the support of these institutions, large demands are made upon the Churches, as such, or upon their more able members, and when these demands are presented, the appeals are quite apt to be addressed to denominational pride or prejudice. "The ——— are doing generously for *their* Academy or College, and *they* are reaping the benefits. *We* must contribute more nobly to ours, or it will suffer in the comparison, and *our* interests will be injuriously affected." Thus, while we are all the

[1] See Dr. Wayland's "Thoughts on the present Collegiate System in the United States."

friends of education, we are expected to favor it in such forms and in such relations as that the advantages will inure to ourselves.

Now, placing out of the account the moral effect of such competition, it will be obvious that, by supporting more institutions than are needed, Christians are perpetrating a sinful waste of their means of usefulness. Churches are robbed of pastors to supply presidents and professors, while many, who might be pastors or evangelists, are detained as instructors in small, sickly institutions. And then the amount of funds that is annually drawn from the Churches to relieve these institutions from embarrassment, or to sustain their half-famished existence, is no small item of expenditure, and might be more judiciously appropriated. I may be told that more is done in this way, than would be accomplished under any system of Christian union. Probably more is *given*, but is more *done?* And are sectarian motives necessary to impel Christians to a due liberality? It may be true, according to Quarles, that

> "Some faiths are like those mills that cannot grind
> Their corn, unless they work against the wind;"

and it may be true that some men are the most profuse in their donations under the provocatives of opposition; but it is none the less true that under this system there is an enormous mispplication of resources.

As circumstances are, human wisdom cannot easily determine how this evil may be remedied. It is the natural fruit of our divisions and their consequent jealousies and rivalries, and, by a reäcting process, aggravates the cause in which it originated. The curse belongs to the spirit of schism, and there must the corrective be applied.

We are accustomed to speak of the destitutions of our country. Large tracts of moral territory are represented as unreclaimed, and inviting the care and the toil of the evangelical cultivator. And so long as the divisions, which few attempt to heal, are perpetuated, will these moral wastes be likely to remain and to enlarge themselves, reproaching us for our selfishness, and giving to the winds their cry for relief. We have places of worship enough, and preachers enough, in the evangelical denominations of this country, to supply double the territory and double the population, that are now accommodated, with the means of grace. There is not an economical distribution, and the cause of this inequality will be found mainly in the fact, — not, as some suppose, that the cities and large towns are excessively supplied with preachers and places of worship,—but that the spirit of sect has prevented diffusion by crowding two, three, or more Churches and as many preachers into small places, where a single Church and a single pastor could and should have occupied the whole ground.

Of course, all denominations have an equal right to establish Churches, build houses of worship, and support preachers wherever they please, on territory lawfully procured, accountable only to the Judge of all for their motives, their principles, or their policy. The question with which we are just now concerned is not one of simple natural right,—for, touching that point, there is little difference of opinion; nor is it one of mere Christian comity, respecting which there is, unhappily, much laxity of conscience,—but it is a question of expediency, of practical wisdom, of prudent economy, such as concerns all who would do the greatest good with their means, and do it under a full sense of their accountability to Christ. Is it becoming Christians so to differ as to bring their efforts into collision, and make their natural rights reciprocally destructive? Is it a judicious distribution of their men and money, to appropriate more than are needed to a small field, when whole regions, measured by miles rather than by acres, are totally neglected? Take a village which, with its immediate surroundings, contains three hundred or five hundred inhabitants. One house of worship, of moderate dimensions, could accommodate all who might attend. One minister could preach to the whole, and perform all the duties that properly belong to a pastor. But what is more common than to see, in such a village, two or more houses of worship, with each its vestry for social meetings, and each its bell, heavy enough to be heard by other villages, and each its preacher, a little better, it is contended, than the other or others. Now, setting aside, for the present, the bad moral influence which, from humiliating observation, we know is the almost invariable attendant of such a state of things, let any one estimate for himself the loss to the general cause which results mainly from that fruitful source of evil, sectarian division. All the preachers, more than one, might be spared for destitute districts. All the money expended, beyond the sum required for one set of ecclesiastical operations, might have been given to the aid of feebler Churches, or the promotion of Home Missions, or in various other ways, to advance the general cause.

Nor is this want of economy the whole of the evil. Where there are so many societies for so few people, they are necessarily small and feeble. Their houses of worship, erected under the influence of sectarian pride and competition, often cost them more than they can pay, and they are compelled to provide for the interest of a debt, or to call upon Churches in other places for relief from the incumbrance. They cannot adequately support the preachers they want, and are obliged to borrow or beg to make up for a deficiency, or to employ, at lower rates, preachers of inferior ability, and, as a consequence, lose their more intelligent hearers. Under this system, to a large extent, have grown up two evils, — begging for meeting-houses, and instability of the pastoral relation, — evils which no grand jury has yet presented as nuisances.

Thus, in consequence of our sectarian disunion, our resources, both physical and spiritual, are absorbed in the accomplishment of sectarian objects. We are "consumed one of another," and little is left for the higher ends of the Christian life. There, flaming out on the inspired page, is the unfulfilled, unrepealed command, "Go ye into all the world, and preach the gospel to every creature." But, no; we cannot do that: for the little vineyards which we have been trying to enlarge, a yard per annum, cannot spare us, or more than a pittance of our property. Two, three, four of us, all evangelical in the main, must take care of our respective fractions of a village, come what will of hundreds of millions who never heard the first word of the gospel! No; we cannot contribute for any outside objects, — often this is sober fact, — for we have such heavy expenses in supporting *our* society, that we stagger under our burden! Is this right? Can any unperverted conscience think it right? The differences among evangelical denominations may have their importance. My argument requires not their depreciation. But are they so important as to justify this doubling and trebling of our forces in such small fields, when seven-eighths of earth's population are perishing in ignorance and guilt? Are no personal comforts to be surrendered, no desirable gratifications to be sacrificed, for the benefit of millions hastening to the pagan's grave and the pagan's eternity?

This multiplication of feeble societies has also an unfavorable effect upon the intellectual character of the ministry. A cry from the heathen, or from the destitute regions of our own country, seldom withdraws a candidate for the sacred vocation from his studies. The call may be loud and piercing, but it is not heard; or, if heard, not heeded. He feels the need of thorough training; he must endeavor to qualify himself more fully for his important work. In all this he may be right. But, let an application come from some village where are two or more rival interests, all acknowledged to be essentially Christian; and let him be told that the "other societies" have each a pastor; that *his* denomination are suffering exceedingly from their destitution; that the young people are going off to the other meetings; that the choir and the Sabbath School are diminishing, — and a chord is touched that vibrates, and none the less because he may have in prospect certain domestic arrangements. His sectarian feelings are brought into full play; denominational interests are depending upon his decision; and it requires but a few more facts of the same bearing, and a little more entreaty from the deacon or the committee, commissioned to negotiate with him, to overcome his love of study, and conquer all his scruples touching his obligations to the Education Society or other patrons, and to make him forego the advantages of a thorough course which he has often spoken of as too important to be sacrificed. The little society of seventy-five or a hundred must be taken care of, and he is *the* man to guard their interests against all depredators. The duties will not be severe; he can there pursue his studies, and, on the whole, perhaps, get as much good as by continuing a few years longer in his well-begun course. He accepts the invitation, marries, is ordained, flourishes a while the wonder of the village. Five years afterwards, where is he, and what is he?

As we look through the land, we see not a few, any one of whom might have sat for this picture; and every one of whom is a standing proof of the injurious influence of sectarian divisions and rivalries. These divisions and competitions, by practically reducing the standard of ministerial attainments, rob the Church of a large amount of ministerial power. If it be said that this evil is not universal among the denominations, I reply, that gratitude is due to God for the preservation of any from its baneful effects.

I might proceed further, specifying particulars of perversion and waste of the energies of the Church resulting from her unholy divisions. But need I say more? How, my brother, can the Church of Christ consent to such an appropriation of resources that were given her by her Lord for other and nobler purposes? How can she afford thus to squander so much of her strength, when the whole, most carefully economized, is only sufficient for the purposes specified in her charter of incorporation? And why does she persist in cherishing and perpetuating the reign of that spirit of evil — Schism — a demon whose motto, worn on his brow in sulphureous characters, is — *Divide and destroy!*

3. THE INJURIOUS EFFECT OF DIVISION IN WEAKENING THE DEMONSTRATION IN FAVOR OF OUR RELIGION.

When Jesus stood at the grave of Lazarus, he prayed to his Father, as if for permission to raise his friend to life, and assigned as a reason, that he wished to convince the spectators of the divinity of his mission: "Because of the people that stand by I said it, that they may believe that thou hast sent me." And, after predicting a future event, he added, "Now I tell you before it come, that when it is come to pass, ye may believe that I am he." Standing alone in the world, he was obliged to furnish proofs in himself that he was the Sent of the Father, the Saviour long promised, long expected. To this end he employed miracle and prophecy, as the best adapted, in his circumstances, to produce the desired conviction. But, when he was about to leave the world, he selected another kind of evidence, that should be permanent and intelligible proof of the Divine origin of his religion. Addressing his followers, he had said: "By this shall all men know that ye are my disciples, if ye have love one to another;" thus indicating the way by which the world should ascertain their relation to their Master. But, addressing his Father in that prayer which he may have intended as a specimen of his sacerdotal intercession, he said: "Neither pray I for these alone, but for them also which shall believe on me through their word; THAT THEY ALL MAY BE ONE; as thou, Father, art in me, and I in thee, that they also may be ONE IN US; THAT THE WORLD MAY BELIEVE THAT THOU HAST SENT ME." And again, immediately after: "The glory which thou gavest me, I have given them; that THEY MAY BE ONE, even as we are one; I in them, and thou in me, that they may be made PERFECT IN ONE; and THAT THE WORLD MAY KNOW THAT THOU HAST SENT ME, and hast loved them as thou hast loved me." This oneness of Christians would be something new, and would attract attention. Nothing of the kind had appeared in any form of society, and the Saviour knew that human nature would never produce an association of unrelated individuals bound together entirely by love. There was nothing analogous to it in paganism, or even judaism. A people drawn together from all nations and all classes; of all possible temperaments, all gradations of intelligence, all diversities of custom; and so subdued and assimilated in their moral feelings as to constitute a unity, having "one heart and one soul," — would indeed be something extraordinary, — a moral wonder, such as the world had never seen, and such as would carry conviction to the most reluctant and sceptical of the presence and prevalence of a supernatural agency.

In this exhibition by Christ of a great principle, we have a key that opens to us, in part at least, the secret of the astonishing success of the early Christians. "Union is strength," says every one capable of articulating a truism; and when it is uttered, the main idea is doubtless physical. Rivers united form the mighty Mississippi. Snow-flakes united form the irresistible avalanche. Atoms united form the mountain barrier. Battalions united form the victorious army. States and provinces united make the powerful empire. But who remembers that the mere fact of union may in itself, apart from all action, be power? Entirely apart from the aggressive movements of the primitive Christians, — apart from all their preaching, exhorting, praying, — there was an unconscious influence acting upon observers; their affectionate harmony, their oneness of spirit, produced upon the world impressions favorable to their character and to the claims of their religion. As the result of the union, multitudes were led to think better, not only of them, but also of their Master, and to open their minds the more candidly and receptively to their heavenly message. Tertullian says that this fact commanded the attention of their enemies, and called forth expressions of admiration;[1] and he reckons the brotherly love and concord of the Church among the primary elements of her moral power. Gibbon, whose principal work is envenomed with subtle sneers and malignant satires, aimed at a religion which he hated the more the less he understood it, — even Gibbon, in his attempts to account for the rapid propagation of early Christianity, — a fact which he admits and endeavors to explain without an acknowledgment of any superhuman agency, — assigns a number of causes, and this as one of the most efficient — the union that subsisted among Christians. Poor man! why did he not, in a manly spirit, examine the nature and the causes of that remarkable union? He perceived the relation of the two facts as antecedent and consequent. Christians were affectionately united, and therefore were successful wherever they went with their message. What was the antecedent of the former fact, the Christian union to which such results were largely attributable? There was a department of truth which depravity was afraid to approach, and the intellect, restrained

[1] "Vide, inquiunt, ut se diligunt; et pro alterutro mori parati sunt."

by the heart, left it untouched. Therein was evidence of the Divine origin of the Christian system, and to call that witness would be fatal to his case.

Be it remembered, that so long as Christians remained united, with their ranks compact, and their efforts directed to the conversion of the world, the Church commanded the world's respect, and she went on increasing in numbers and strength. But the moment the spirit of schism found admission, and she became divided, and turned her weapons against portions of herself, she was dishonored in the eyes of the world, her progress was retarded, the beginnings of her imbecility were apparent, and she ceased to be a reliable witness for Christ.

The innumerable divisions and bitter controversies that defaced the beauty and crippled the energy of the Christian Church during the fourth, fifth, and sixth centuries, prepared the way for the successes of the false prophet of Mecca, and facilitated the triumphs of that system of imposture which, even now, has more adherents than the Christianity of the New Testament. "While the Church was one," says Isaac Taylor, "Christianity spread, or, should we not say, burst over the world, and gathered myriads of converts from lands within and far beyond the limits of the Roman empire. When Christians became factious, when other names than the name of Christ were called upon, then the evangelical circle drew in apace: no more conquests were made; or they were conquests purely nominal; and, ere long, the fierce Avenger of the Lord's quarrel with his Church, breaking bounds, sword in hand, from his sultry Arabian sands, drove the distracted flock from field to field, until the Christian name was near to be quite lost from the world."[1]

Who that has ever conversed with a papist, or read a Romish book, is not aware that a standing objection to Protestantism is its want of unity? "You," says the Romanist, "are not one. You are divided in creed, in ritual, in organization, in feeling. In all these respects the Catholic Church is one. Agree among yourselves in faith, in communion, in action, before you ask us even to examine your theory." However remote from the truth may be the declaration that the Catholic Church is so completely one, and however objectionable may be her seeming unity, resulting, as it does, from the pressure of an unparalleled spiritual despotism, still the argument is valid,

[1] Saturday Evening, pp. 336–7.

so far as it applies to Protestantism; and Protestants should know and feel that, by continuing their schisms and dissensions, they are contributing to the perpetuity of a system of error and superstition which they profess to abhor, and riveting the fetters of the papacy upon millions of enslaved souls, for whose redemption they profess to pray and labor.[1]

The quarrels and alienations that prevailed among the Reformers of the sixteenth century, impeded the progress of the Reformation, and many who sincerely desired its success, were so grieved at heart by these unchristian strifes, that they never withdrew from the mother Church. And, ever since, not a year has passed but this same argument has carried many a proselyte over to Popery; and that argument — call it as you please, fair or foul, legitimate or sophistical—is at this moment successfully urged over the whole

[1] "The Papal body, weak in its utter want of Scriptural support, — weak in its idolatries, its practical enormities, and its plain hostility to the Word of God, — is yet strong in one thing only, that it moves as a single phalanx, obedient to a single will. Whatever it wins, it wins simply through our divisions. That immense mass which embraces most of the manhood of our country, stands, in the presence of these divisions, uncertain, embarrassed, indifferent, or, at least, inactive."— *Bishop Burgess.*

territory of Protestant Christendom; and never shall we deprive it of power for evil until we can show that we are truly one, not only in our protests against the abominations of the Man of Sin, but also in our views of truth, our Christian practice, and our fraternal coöperation.

Infidelity, too, has availed itself of our divisions to barb and poison the shafts which it has aimed at the life of Christianity. This, it may be said, and said truly, it has done disingenuously and maliciously; but the fact remains unaltered, that we have furnished fatal occasion to the disingenuous and malicious to pierce and inflame, perpetrating damage which the tears of all living Christians can never efface, and which the labors of many generations of the holiest can never repair. It was well said by an eminent writer of the seventeenth century, and it is still deplorably true, that "our controversies about religion have brought even religion itself into controversy."[1] And our attempts to apologize for our diversities of religious sentiment and practice, by the alleged obscurity of Scripture and the consequent innocence of contradicting interpreters, have only

[1] Stillingfleet's Irenicum: A Weapon-Salve for the Church's Wounds.

aggravated the evil by virtually justifying the rejection of a Book that is so equivocal and susceptible of such a variety of constructions.

It is also matter of painful experience, that our efforts for the conversion of the impenitent, who are not professed infidels, are the more ineffective in consequence of our divisions. Even though we abstain from disputes and criminations, yet the simple fact of our distribution into sects, with every one its lines of intrenchments, and its posted sentinels, and its system of watchwords, is held up by the unbeliever as a protective shield against every argument, every appeal. Says Dr. Carson: "The differences that subsist among Christians are among the chief obstacles to the progress of the gospel. Scoffers triumph in our divisions, and the world in general are stumbled. By the existence of so many religious sects, unbelievers are prejudiced against the truth; and believers who are blended with worldly Churches, are kept from considering the duty of separation."[1] How often, in our conversation with individuals, is this fact presented by them in resistance of our tenderest expostulations; so that we make no progress till, after an awkward attempt at explanation which seldom satisfies ourselves, we have

[1] Reply to Dr. Ewing, 1809.

extorted a reluctant, half-way concession that, as sinners, they need a Saviour, and that Christ is the Saviour they need. We allege, with truth, that men act irrationally when they assign this fact as a reason why they should not honor the claims of personal religion. As well might they say that they would not love their country, and obey its laws, because there are rival and conflicting parties in politics. As well might they refuse to dine until all the clocks in town strike twelve together. Their conduct in this matter is inexcusably deficient in manliness, and tends to self-ruin. The fault which they perversely employ to their own destruction, is the fault of Christians, and not of the Christianity that requires of all repentance, faith, and a holy life. But still the evil is none the less real or pernicious, because sinners perversely employ it to their own undoing. We blame them for the suicide, and yet supply the weapon with which we know they may insanely take the life of their souls. Constituted as man is, we can never prevent the consequent until we withdraw the well-known antecedent. And here, my brother, let me refer you to an excellent charge by Bishop Burgess to the clergy of his diocese. One paragraph I cannot forbear to quote:

"There is a blessing which, could it be attained,

would remove one of the most prevailing obstacles to cordial conviction, and would leave to the Gospel such power as it has not known for centuries. It is the blessing of Unity. If you ask of twenty different men, as you meet them, their reason for delaying or refusing obedience to the commands of Christianity, ten of them, if not fifteen, will ask in return how they can be expected to see clearly where guides so differ, and where sects and churches contend with such eagerness. With the reasonableness or even sincerity of this reply we are not now concerned; but it is lamentable that it can be made and cannot be refuted. It is a spectacle that should arouse the Christians of this land, and compel all idle strife, at least, to be silent. All of us feel the evil; but most of us despair of a remedy, till the mighty Spirit of God shall cause us to see eye to eye, and produce an uniformity of persuasion, which till now has not existed, since at the Reformation the Bible was thrown open. To indulge in idle projects would indeed avail little; yet, amongst the many speculations of our time, few might be more harmless than those which should be directed towards Christian union and unity; and if some sagacious minds were employed in actual efforts for its attainment, the recollection would not be bitter to them in advancing years, nor would the story be told with dishonor in coming ages. It is time that this weapon were withdrawn from the hands of the enemy."

It is no unusual thing for the strifes and conflicts of two or more denominations whose differences of creed are not great, to give birth to organized forms of fatal error, and to supply the nutriment by which they thrive and overgrow the products of evangelical truth. Noxious vegetation rises into the rankest luxuriance on battle-fields where the soil is enriched by the blood and bones of fallen combatants. Show me the spots, on either hemisphere, where Christians have the most fiercely battered and bruised one another, or where they who had every reason for living peaceably together have indulged in petty controversies about secondary interests, and I will show you the spots where the worst errors are the most deeply rooted and bear the most poisonous fruits.

In your journeying you come in sight of a beautiful valley, in which, along a single street, is a village of a hundred houses, some of stone, some of brick, but mostly of wood, and interspersed with the offices of professional men, the stores of merchants, the shops of artisans, and school-houses. Through that valley meanders a stream that has its head in a mountain lake, and is for miles a brawling torrent, dashing wildly over rocks and dams, and affording power for the driving of productive machinery; but here it quietly moves between banks that are dotted with clumps of bushes, and shaded by many a stately elm or button-wood. The valley is skirted on both sides by hills, whose sides are highly cultivated, and at whose bases are gentle slopes and alluvial meadows richly burdened with the green or the golden products of industry waving in the western breeze. From the summit of one of these hills you contemplate the scene, and admire. Surely, you think, Johnson must have stood here before he wrote that luscious description of "The Happy Valley." Behind you are mountains through whose passes you have threaded your way; across the valley, in the blue distance, are other mountains whose precipitous sides you are to climb to-morrow. But you are thinking of neither the past nor the future; you are enchanted by the present. The vale at your feet, rich in natural beauty, has derived from art additional loveliness; and, as you gaze, you wonder if the Old World can furnish a view of equal charms. From the midst of the cluster of dwellings, now embowered in the richest mid-summer foliage, there loom up in dignified prominence three edifices, differing in shape, dimensions, and color, and you at once recognize them as devoted to the worship of Almighty God.

Not knowing the extent of the population in the vicinity, and supposing, quite naturally, that the supply is created by actual demand, you conclude that the moral scenery before you is only the counterpart of the physical. "Happy people!" you exclaim; "how liberal the provision for thy spiritual culture! Here, surely, Piety has her cherished home! Here the fruits of holiness abound! And if there be contention in heaven, it must be as to who of all

> 'The spirits in bliss
> Shall bow their bright wings to a scene such as this,'

and here fulfil their ministry to the heirs of salvation!"

I grieve, my brother, to break that delicious enchantment. But what says history? Within the memory of the middle-aged there was in that village but one place of worship, and that was of sufficient capacity to accommodate all in the township. Its pulpit was respectably filled by a man of unquestioned piety, and sound evangelical principles; and of his impartiality and industry as a pastor no one had occasion to complain. In process of time, another denomination, differing by only a few faint shades from the former, found favor with some of the people, and a house of worship was erected, partly by foreign aid, and a preacher of fair ability was settled. The result, of course, was division, followed by a perturbed state of the social elements, warm discussion, acrimonious debate, calumnious reports, irritated feelings, disruption of friendships, embittered alienations, and all the unlovely effects of partisan warfare. These two Churches agreed in everything fundamental to the soul's salvation; and yet, as you have often seen illustrated, the strength of their antipathy seemed to be inversely as the square of their distance theologically from each other. Each minister regarded himself as "set for the defence" of those points in which he differed from the other, and to them he devoted many a week of study and many a carefully prepared sermon. Their adherents, with belligerent heads, and hearts, and tongues, rallied around their respective leaders, and pushed them on to the conflict. A proselyting spirit became rife; and if an individual changed sides, he was hailed by the favored party as an important acquisition, and decried by the deserted party as no loss to be regretted. If, by the great grace of God, a person was converted, he was sure to be visited by both ministers, and all the deacons, and no pains were spared, on either side, to induce him to join "*our* Church." If a new family came to reside in the place, they were invited to attend "*our* meeting," and by both parties inducements were offered, such as a pew furnished, exemption from taxes, and even denominational patronage in secular business. All this was accompanied by abundance of complimentary remarks touching *our* minister, *our* meeting-house, *our* singing, *our* Sabbath School, and the class of people in *our* congregation; and as certainly by a superabundance of detractive hints with respect to everything pertaining to the other society. At length, one of the societies concluded to erect a new house of worship, and the subscription for the purpose, though deficient by one third of the estimated cost, was so large that few, without inconvenience, could redeem their pledges. A spacious edifice, with a lofty steeple, was erected and dedicated, with a heavy mortgage upon it. A bell, the largest in the county, was mounted in the belfry, and for a whole day was made to send its echoes among the hills, taunting, with iron tongue, the humbled and mortified occupants of the smaller and less fashionable sanctuary. This was too much to be quietly endured. The pride of sect was touched in a tender point, and it was at once resolved not to be outdone, but to outdo. Another season the other society would have a meeting-house a little better than the boasted best. They were as good as their word; for what cannot the sectarian spirit do?—what, except influence mankind to love God and one another? No matter for the expense; no matter for a debt which should hang for years to their neck like a millstone; no matter for anything but successful rivalry. The corner stone was laid with a flourish; the house went up, one foot longer and six inches wider than the other.[1] The steeple stretched its triangular points two feet farther towards the physical heavens than its far-reaching neighbor. A bell ten pounds heavier than the other, and of "*much* better tone," was balanced aloft, and for many a noisy hour was made to retort the provocation which had been neither forgiven nor forgotten. Well! there they are, two large and beautiful houses, either of sufficient capacity for the wants of the entire population. The one has green blinds on the outside, and the other is frescoed inside; the one has a rosewood pulpit, and the other has an organ; the one has gothic windows, and the other has a colonnade in front. The preachers prepare their ablest discourses, the bells are rung, and the people collect, eyeing one another askance as they pass in opposite directions; but seldom is either house more than one-third filled with hearers.

[1] I know two church edifices, thus built in rivalry, where the dimensions differed only *one inch* each way.

Just at this point a man of great self-assurance and a flippant tongue comes along, and appoints a Sabbath service in the school-house, where he proposes to advocate a system of doctrine derived from any source other than the Word of God. For several years there had been a few individuals in the place who were inclined to that belief, and who, in the midst of the strifes that had raged around them, had acquired increased dislike of evangelical religion and its professors. The meeting was fully attended, and the preacher was invited to leave another appointment. His theory was captivating; he made the way of life broad, and heaven of easy attainment. The result was, that within a year a society was formed around this man, whom both the preëxistent societies agreed, without meaning to agree, to pronounce "an intruder." Many, disgusted with the dissensions by which the community had been lacerated and inflamed, readily fell into the new organization, knowing little and caring less what tenets or morals they might be encouraging. The young people, attracted by novelty as well as by the license to sin which the new doctrine gave them, were inclined in that direction; and thus, by various means, the third party were strengthened and soon enabled to provide a temple of their own. In the meantime, the two Churches, led on by their ministers, reproached and criminated each other as the occasion of this pestilent intrusion, damaging to both; and the belligerent spirit took on new forms, only to alienate still more of their supporters and turn the balance against themselves by supplying recruits to the common enemy.

> "The peaceful Spirit, like a dove,
> Flies from the realms of noise and strife."

In that community, practical godliness is little known. Revivals have been infrequent, very limited in extent, very superficial, very equivocal in the character of their fruits. The few who love the truth are disheartened, and the people generally are the contemners of Christ and his claims.

That, my enamored brother, is the moral interior of a scene upon which you are lavishing your encomiums; and, while you are so benevolently fancying that it must be the favorite resort of the heavenly visitants, the angel of the pit is there, flapping his dark wings over the place, and screaming, in irony, "See, how these Christians love one another!"

This sketch, if compared with the state of things in many communities, may justly be considered as exaggerated; but, in its general features, it answers for hundreds of places, fairly exhibiting the practical workings of the sectarian spirit, and showing how disastrous are its effects, not only upon Christian character, but Christian usefulness. Multitudes are disaffected, then filled with prejudices, then alienated from public worship, and made the easy prey of "seducing spirits that lie in wait to deceive," and lead their victims in a mass to perdition. Even if the prejudiced and repelled assume no organized form, and rally around no heretical standard, they become the despisers of the Christian profession, the contemners of experimental religion, the open violaters of the Sabbath, the scornful neglecters of all the means of grace, and, so far as human agency is concerned, utterly unapproachable, invulnerable. The question is, indeed, a fearful one: Where lies the responsibility? We may lay the whole at the door of human depravity; but whence comes the aliment upon which depravity and error thus fatten and thrive? One party, and another party, may say, "We are not in the fault." Satan takes care, for the present, to reproach none of us, and pronounces us his most efficient coädjutors. But what is the decision of Him, who says, "See that ye love one another with a pure heart fervently?" All parties, and certainly all persons, may not be equally culpable; but which is the denomination to whom, in this department, he might not say, "I have somewhat against thee?"

All the sects, properly entitled to the name of Christian, are engaged, with more or less zeal, in efforts to propagate the gospel among the heathen, — a service quite similar in its aims to that which proved the devotedness, and absorbed the resources, of the primitive Church. But, unlike to that Church, they are going forth in separate bands, with every one its distinctive name, system of belief, and mode of ecclesiastical organization. Considerable success has attended the labors of them all, and all have now their Churches composed of converts from heathenism. It is not apparent that God has made any distinction in the matter of success, on the ground of their denominational peculiarities. They preach Christ, and the Holy Spirit gives them souls renewed as the fruits of their fidelity. For the present, the converts are happily ignorant of Protestant schisms. But not very remote is the day when they will become acquainted with the discreditable fact, that those who have so benevolently come thousands of miles to impart to them the gospel, are divided among themselves; that they interpret differently some parts of the Book which they allege to be inspired; and that those who sent and support them are separated into sects which refuse to coöperate, and are not on terms of cordial fellowship. Naturally inquisitive, they will inquire into the facts, and insist upon explanation. How shall they be satisfied? It will be a sad day for the missionary, when he must disclose the real truth, and make an effort to transform his simple-hearted brethren from Christians into sectarians. They have read in their own tongue the Gospels and the Epistles, so kindly translated for them, and the impression thence derived is that believers in Christ are one. The lessons and the petitions of Jesus upon this subject they have committed to memory. The picture drawn by Luke of the unanimity and affection of the primitive Church, has filled them with admiration. The teachings of the Apostles, with respect to brotherly love and mutual forbearance, they have regarded as beautifully adapted to produce upon earth a miniature heaven. But facts are now developed, strangely at variance with the impressions which they have received from the New Testament. They learn the state of things in those far-off lands which the missionaries, for their sakes, have left behind. They become acquainted, too, with the differences, both of belief and practice, that exist among the missionaries of the various denominations. They are startled; they are perplexed; they are grieved. "Is Christ divided?" "No, no;" is the prompt, unanimous reply. "Why, then, are *you* divided? Why are *we* divided? Whence these party names? If there be but one Lord, why are there more than one faith and one baptism?" These questions will yet be proposed, and all missionaries must be prepared to meet them. Who can foresee the results? Will none of the converts acquire from their explaining teachers either the spirit or the tactics of party? Will none of them lose confidence in their new-found religion, and decline in their zeal for its diffusion among their countrymen? And when the unconverted heathen shall come to learn the facts as they are, will they not, more captiously than ever, object to an exchange of their religion for another whose character and tendencies are thus practically exhibited? A valuable American missionary, foreseeing this inevitable evil, has proposed a rule of action to be observed by all sects, which, he thinks, would result in the greatest benefit to the Church and the world. "In selecting their spheres of action," says Mr. Abeel, "let each denomination pass by the places already occupied, and fix upon those where their services are most needed. Let it be a mutual understanding, that if education or predilection dispose the inhabitants of any part of a country to a particular sect, all others will yield the ground." There is plausibility in this proposal; it is kind in spirit; and you, my brother, will inquire why the experiment should not first be tried in our home-field. But creditably courteous as would be such an arrangement for the distribution of heathen territory, it would only postpone the development of facts which must ultimately be known, and the result would be such an extension of our divisions, geographically, as would greatly diminish the feasibility, and render more remote the prospect, of an ultimate and happy adjustment of our differences. Perhaps the excellent brother who expects from the application of this rule "the most desirable consequences," anticipates that before there should be any actual infringement by one denomination upon the territory of another, the predicted and looked-for millennial period will have arrived, in which shall be restored the glad scenes of primitive harmony and fellowship. Happy anticipation! But, alas! how ill adapted to the production of universal fraternity and concord is the process of extending party lines, till, like the great circles of the astronomer, they shall not only encompass the globe, but reach the heavens! What progress are we likely to make towards the desirable union, while the walls of separation are continually strengthened, every party fortifying them on its own side?

The injurious tendency of our sectarian divisions, to which I now refer as likely to be developed in the field of our Foreign Missionary operations, is painfully apprehended by many of the missionaries themselves, — by all who are placed in circumstances that direct their attention to the subject. Where laborers of different denominations occupy the same field, as in large cities, and have formed Churches side by side, they have felt so deeply the importance of producing upon all around the conviction of their substantial oneness, as to be constrained to pursue a line of conduct to which they had never been accustomed at home, and for which they have supposed it not improbable they might incur the animadversion of their distant supporters. I do not suggest a suspicion that they have acted insincerely, or that they have sacrificed the convictions of conscience upon the altar of expediency. They were honest before God, and did what they were sure would be pleasing to him. I mention the fact merely to show how deep is the impression upon the minds of those who are in circumstances to appreciate the argument, that the divisions among Christians are unfavorable to their influence over the heathen.

No Christian, I presume, desires that the piety of the present generation of believers should be transferred to the pagan world. On the contrary, it is matter of fervent prayer that the mould into which the converts from heathenism might be cast, should be more after the primitive pattern, including all the elements of a higher order of piety than ours; a stronger faith, a deeper humility, a warmer love, a greater deadness to the world, and a fuller consecration of all to Christ. Is any Christian willing to have the sectarian divisions with which we are familiar, extended to Asia, Africa, and the Isles of the Sea, and to have reënacted there the competitions and strifes of Protestant Europe and America? The idea is to me inexpressibly painful and revolting; and, while I would ask no body of Christians to intermit their efforts for the evangelization of the heathen, but would urge them onward by all the motives which can be derived from the command of Christ, the value of the soul, and the retributions of eternity, I would, nevertheless, importune them, by the love of the Saviour, and by their duty to posterity, not to transfer to pagan lands, and therefore not to perpetuate at home, an evil so manifestly unchristian, and so fatally charged with pernicious elements.

I may be reminded that the various denominations, however divided and debilitated, are doing much and purposing to do more for the conversion of the world; and that, notwithstanding their disunion, God blesses their endeavors, and makes their labors effective, so that in no century since the decease of the apostles has Christianity achieved such extensive triumphs as we are permitted to witness. All this is readily conceded; and with any brother I will bow my knees in devout gratitude to the God of all grace for every fact which he may produce from this department. But if he wishes me to conclude from such premises that our schisms are not seriously interfering with our Christian efficiency, and may be tolerated as a minor evil, I must respectfully plead *non sequitur*, and remonstrate with him, not only for the illegitimacy of his logic, but also for the objectionable condition of his moral feelings. He is not ignorant of what the New Testament requires of Christians as to both spirit and conduct. He knows the validity of the argument drawn from the extraordinary successes of the primitive, missionary, united Church. He is aware that, mainly as a consequence of our divisions and controversies, Mohammedanism, Popery, and Irreligion still divide the more enlightened portions of the world among themselves. He can number the disciples of reformed Christianity, and learn for himself that they still remain an insignificant minority. He will surely admit that the spirit of disunion, "by confirming the irreligious in their impiety, disheartening the sincere inquirer after truth, and blinding numbers with the idea that the sectarian spirit is true piety, is still ruinous to the souls of men; and that, by dividing our limited instrumentality at home, and tending to counteract our Christian influence abroad, and, incomparably more than all, by grieving the Holy Spirit of God, it is still enfeebling and endangering our missionary operations, and delaying the conversion of the world."[1] And will he deliberately suggest considerations to show the comparative harmlessness or innocence of an evil that he ought to condemn? Will he plead for mitigation of sentence, or ask me to soften the tone of unqualified rebuke? He and I are involved in the consequences of this evil. May we not be responsible for its continuance!

Both in this country and in Europe I have heard addresses upon anniversary platforms, in which very charming things were said touching the "incidental benefits of sectarian rivalries and competitions;" and could I have felt that the

[1] Rev. Dr. Harris's Prize Essay on Christian Union.

speakers were not obsequiously flattering those with whom they refused all visible fellowship, and were not endeavoring to relieve themselves from the conscious awkwardness of a position of seeming union to which their previous conduct supplied no fair counterpart, and with which they did not expect that their future course would harmonize, I should have had more respect for their sincerity, and probably been more enraptured by their declamation. Incidental benefits of sectarian rivalries and competitions! Fine theme for a Christian minister when facing an audience of thousands, and pleading the claims of the crucified Saviour, the obligations of his redeemed and consecrated Church, and the wants of millions perishing in sin! Apologizing for a wrong which Christ abhors, which for fifteen centuries has been the deformity and disgrace of Christianity, and which is at present, however modified, a prime curse of the Church! How much more consistent with the dignity of his office, and the proprieties of the occasion, to present the Cross, and, taking his own position the nearest to it, summon us by the miseries of humanity, by the solemnities of the judgment, by the woes of the lost, by the felicities of the saved, and more than all, by the agonies and the blood of Calvary, to join him in renewed consecration of body, soul and spirit, time, talent and wealth, to the work of saving a guilty, ruined race! Incidental benefits of division, disunion, alienation among the disciples of Jesus, all jointly and severally expectants of a heavenly inheritance! O, man of God! tell us rather of the blessed effects of unanimity of sentiment, similarity of practice, prevalence of brotherly love, holy consolidation into one Apostolic Church, with one name, one heart, one way, one object, affectionately coöperating in the Master's service. Tell us of that desirable period when the Church shall become all that the prophets predicted, all that the Saviour desired, all that the apostles labored to make her. There is to be such a period, when "the light of the moon shall be as the light of the sun; and the light of the sun seven-fold, as the light of seven days;" and that shall be "IN THE DAY THAT THE LORD BINDETH UP THE BREACH OF HIS PEOPLE, AND HEALETH THE STROKE OF THEIR WOUND." Tell us, servant of Jesus, what shall be the spiritual glories of those "last days," when "the mountain of the Lord's house shall be established on the top of the mountains and exalted above the hills, and all nations shall flow unto it." Tell us of the period of the Church's unity, and what are the signs of its coming. Tell us how she will appear, and what she will do, when she shall be cordially, really one in Christ, her living, ruling Head. "Clothed with the sun," what will be her influence upon a dark and sterile world? Comprehending within herself, by virtue of her union with her Lord, all the elements of moral might; "endued, as of old, with power from on high;" how rapidly will her conquests be achieved, and the seventh angel be permitted to sound, and great voices be heard on high, proclaiming that "the kingdoms of this world are become the kingdoms of our Lord and his Christ, and he shall reign forever and ever!"

III.

SOME METHODS BY WHICH OUR OWN DENOMINATION MAY PROBABLY CONTRIBUTE TO THE PROMOTION OF CHRISTIAN FRATERNITY.

I COME now, dear brother, to the consideration of a branch of my subject that is chiefly practical. Let us again bow together before "the Father of lights," and beseech him, for the Saviour's sake, to bestow upon us liberally that illuminating and sanctifying Influence which alone can lead us into a thorough knowledge of his perfect will, and incline our hearts to do whatsoever may appear to be duty. "The meek will he guide in judgment; and the meek will he teach his way."

I suppose that we, as a denomination, may not take it for granted that we are wholly free from responsibility touching the prevalent disunion of Christians, or that we have nothing to do towards the healing of the breaches that have so long and so injuriously divided the people of God. We may not be wrong to an extent that will require a general or even a partial recession from the trusted platform on which our ecclesiastical organizations have so long immovably reposed. As I have not intermeddled with the fundamental principles of other denominations, so I shall leave ours untouched; and, in pursuing this course, I am influenced, not only by an unwillingness to bring constitutional questions into the discussion, but also by the clear conviction, that, until some previous matters shall have received careful attention, not one of the denominations will be prepared even to examine specific plans of union. Such plans have already been proposed; but, as they have generally commenced with the assumption that the proposing party is right and the others are wrong, they have necessarily failed to win general favor; and this uniform failure, together with some acquaintance with human nature, has led me to the conclusion, that nothing so radical can be accomplished until hearts shall be made better, and tongues more regulated by the law of love, and pens dipped more exclusively in the spirit of Calvary.

By commencing at once those preliminary improvements that shall clear the way to the fundamental elements of a scriptural union, and thus prepare the whole body of believers to perceive the true basis on which Christ would have us harmoniously unite and affectionately coöperate, we may render to ourselves, and, by the force of example, to our brethren of every name, a valuable service. To this end, we should endeavor to obtain distinct and correct views of the deplorable effects of schism, as exhibited in the history of the past, as daily developed in our own times, and as likely to become apparent in the disclosures of the future. Let us conceal nothing from ourselves; let us open our minds to the full impression which the facts will assuredly make upon the considerate and candid. Let us also anticipate, as we certainly may, without any improper license of the imagination, the delightful influence upon the Church and the world of that cordial union which all agree to be desirable. More than all, let us take a midnight walk with Jesus from the table of the Eucharist to the Garden of Sorrows, and, as we passover "the brook in the way," hear him plead for the oneness of his disciples in all lands, all ages of the world. Our minds may thus be made tender and susceptible, and ready to welcome suggestions of a still more definite and practical character.

1. WE MAY ENDEAVOR, CAREFULLY, TO DISPOSSESS OURSELVES OF THE SPIRIT OF SECT.

This spirit I have shown to be the fruitful source of innumerable evils; and, however difficult it may be, so long as Christians retain their sectarian organizations, to dislodge it effectually from their bosoms, yet I know not how, until this be done, they can rationally hope for any thorough, satisfactory reform. Let these organizations be broken up to-day, and, if the spirit that has so long maintained them be not also destroyed, the mass would separate again to-morrow and crystallize afresh around their old centres, as indisposed as ever to a general consolidation. These special affinities, constituting no essential part of Christian character, must yield to the paramount law of cohesion, — the great law of love, — including supreme love to Christ, reverent love to his truth, unreserved love to one another; and then combination will be easy, for it will be natural. The spirit of sect is the principal antagonist to Christian fraternity; for while, by a process all its own, it unites a certain portion, it as surely, by the same process, repels all the remainder. So long, therefore, as it exists in a single mind, there cannot be entire Christian union.

That this spirit has its home among us to a greater extent than in other denominations, I have no reason to believe; but that it exists and operates among us, my observation will not allow me to question. The number who are entirely free from it are, I fear, not a large majority. It crops out at innumerable points, indicating that more is beneath. On almost all occasions, private and public, it is more or less apparent — *l' esprit du corps* — giving cast and coloring to much that is felt, and said, and done. That it is the main-spring of Baptist activity in the religious department, it would be unjust to intimate; but that it is a spring of no small power, we must honestly concede. It is visible in our benevolent operations, our periodical press, our denominational literature, our schools, colleges, and theological institutions; in our men, women, and children; in our prayers, preaching, and almost every form of evangelical effort. It is not, as we are Christians, the principal element of our religious character; but it is, as we are imperfect Christians, an element mingled with and corrupting that which had a better origin. It works covertly, damaging character by the subtle delusion that love of sect is brotherly love, and what we do for sect we do for Christ. We feel so sure that we are right in all respects, as practically to make the kingdom of heaven on earth, and our own denomination one and the same. In this we do not excel others; but, in our measure, we resemble them.

Now, difficult as may be the service here recommended, of removing a spirit that has become incorporated into our nature and habits, so as to seem utterly inextricable, — a spirit to which nutriment is ministered from so many sources; and more difficult as it may be to effect the dislodgement of a spirit of whose presence and malign agency the possessed themselves are not conscious, — still there is no impossibility in the case; for what ought to be done, can be done; and the bare knowledge of the magnitude and heinousness of the evil, and of the incalculable benefits that would result from its thorough repudiation, imposes upon me and you and every Christian the duty of attempting its immediate and entire removal. We should all search our hearts, as the Hebrews searched their dwellings for every remnant of the forbidden leaven; and we should, with perseverance and holy hatred, trace the unhallowed spirit in all its dark and sinuous retreats, and, giving no quarter, seek its complete extermination. The sectarian spirit! What argument can be adduced for its allowed existence in any shape or for any purpose, that may not be pleaded for the perpetuity of schism with all its progeny of abominations? If this spirit, which is the parent and prime nurse of all our disunion, may be spared from annihilation or even reprehension, then may we, then must we spare also our execrations of the divisions which it engenders and nourishes. Tolerate the mother of the diabolical brood, and the offspring will not soon become less numerous or less thrifty.

The spirit of sect is not the spirit of Christ. By

no power of sectarian alchymy can it be transmuted into anything valuable. To the unpractised eye, it may be made to resemble that element of holiness upon which the New Testament so largely insists—*love to the brethren;* but it is the resemblance of a gilded spuriousness to a heaven-coined reality. The more we have of it, the poorer we are; for it not only constitutes no part of the "true riches" of Christian character, but is worse than worthless, occupying that place in the mind which ought to be "filled with all the fulness of God."

Should you inquire what method I would propose for the removal of this wicked spirit, I reply, that we are to put it away as we would any other sinful affection that is deeply rooted. Something may be accomplished by imitating the practical farmer, who kills out the noxious from the soil by planting and cultivating the useful. But, in multitudes of minds, a sterner and more radical process will be requisite; for the vice has struck its tap-root far down into the soul, and its thousand branches and minuter filaments have extended into every department of the moral nature. "Break up your fallow ground, and sow not among thorns." Any one who is acquainted with the natural history of sectarianism, would conclude, *a priori*, that "This kind goeth not out but by prayer and fasting." We must repent before God, and the Church, and the World, that we have ever cherished a spirit so dishonorable to Christianity, so ruinous to souls; and our repentance must be of that effectual kind which uproots and flings away all uncharitableness, and prepares the soul for the full, unobstructed growth of that "perfect love" which takes to its bosom all the good in the universe. And connected with this there must be prayer: "Create in me a clean heart, O God! and renew a right spirit within me."

2. WE MAY CULTIVATE A HIGHER DEGREE OF PERSONAL HOLINESS.

SIN is, in the moral world, the fatal cause of repulsion and separation. It is the occasion of those conflicts which disturb the inward tranquillity of the individual; and to its influence we may trace the disorder and confusion that are everywhere reckoned as social evils. Just in proportion as sin exists in any community, is it impossible to make the moral elements cohere; for its nature is to make men unlike to one another, and therefore unlike to any common standard of character. Hence the inspired declaration — "The founder melteth in vain, for the wicked are not plucked away."

HOLINESS is the great assimilating, combining, cementing principle of the moral world. It harmonizes the faculties and affections of the individual, and produces that internal adjustment and concord which the Scriptures denominate "peace," — "The peace of God which passeth all understanding." So, also, by bringing numbers into harmony with the laws under which God has placed them, and thus conforming them to a common model, holiness makes them resemble one another, and then they come together by the law of simple affinity. Just in proportion, therefore, to the degree of holiness in the members of any social organization, will be the sincerity of their mutual attachment, the strength of their adhesion, and the solidity and indissolubleness of their union. In heaven, the unanimity and the fellowship are perfect, because all the constituents of that happy society are not only sinless, but consciously, actively holy. So, in the Church below, were we "perfect," we should "walk by the same rule, and mind the same thing." Christ is the Source of the attractive power to all his people, whether in the world of glory, or in this state of discipline, drawing them all into oneness around himself; and, as a necessary consequence, the nearer they are to him, the Centre of the moral sphere, the nearer they are to one another.

Who does not know that the more spiritual and heavenly-minded Christians become, the more are they dispossessed of sectarian feelings, and the less easily are they confined within sectarian inclosures? Who has not seen the more devoted and Christ-like of every denomination exhibit their peculiar affinity, by associating for the enjoyment of that endeared communion which they find in familiar conversation upon gracious subjects, and in joint addresses to the throne of heavenly grace? Opposed to everything like schism, and therefore unwilling to draw another dividing line by forming another party, they do not quit their respective Churches, but continue as ever to perform the duties to which they are pledged by covenant relation. But, as opportunity presents, they go to "their own company," to cultivate the friendship of the holiest they can find, and to open their hearts to such as can fully sympathize with their widened views and deepened feelings.

"For the divisions of Reuben there were great searchings of heart." The obstacles that interfere with Christian union may all be referred to one source, the heart. The difficulty, therefore, is moral rather than physical or intellectual, and is to be overcome by moral means — by means directed convergently to the source of the evil. Christians may be brought together, as they are, and induced for a season to coöperate as if sincerely united. A conviction of necessity may apply such pressure as shall procure a mechanical union that shall be of some advantage so long as it lasts. But no sooner is that particular force withdrawn than the elements separate as before, indulging, perhaps, some self-complacency in the faithfulness with which they have observed the truce, and kept the belligerent spirit in temporary abeyance. The union needed is such a union of souls as nothing can effectuate but the heavenly chemistry of holiness, that mighty principle which assimilates hearts and welds them together. How concentrated and combined were the affections of those growing thousands in the primitive Church! "The multitude of them that believed were of ONE HEART." Their purity of character — made such by the baptism of fire — contributed to their union, and their warm fraternal fellowship supplied facilities for still higher attainments in the divine life. "Great grace was upon them all."

To this point, then, we ought to give immediate and earnest attention, for really it is a matter of primary interest. Serious as are the obstacles to the growth of individual piety which are interposed by the divisions of Christians, and especially by the prevalent spirit of sect, still they are not insuperable. Thousands who have worn the party name, and sustained the party relation, have thrown from them the shackles of all party spirit, and risen superior to all party influences, and walked on high with God, in sweet companionship with the holy of all ages and all communions. But it is impossible that Christians, with their present measure of piety, should become generally one. They have too little disinterested love. Their conformity to their blessed Head is too incomplete. They have within them too many sinful elements to admit of happy, permanent cohesion. These elements, such as pride, selfishness, love of the world, emulation, self-esteem, and numerous concomitant evils of a partially sanctified nature, must be thoroughly extirpated from individual minds before they can be qualified candidates for such fellowship as Christ and his apostles commended. That union does not subsist in any denomination — certainly not in ours. We agree in some things; but we are not one according to the New Testament pattern. I question if true gospel unity can be found in any Church of an hundred members on the face of the earth. No church, no denomination is yet within itself holy enough to make its own unanimity more than approximate. Allowing, therefore, that our creed and practice and ecclesiastical polity are preëminently scriptural, and that all denominations of Christians, as the result of intelligent conviction, should adopt them, and thus occupy with us a common platform, there would not, there could not, be true gospel union. We are not united among ourselves; they are not united among themselves. A conjunction of any number of disunited bodies would never make one accordant and harmonious compound. Let us not deceive ourselves. The holiness of the denominations — our own holiness — is not yet such as to justify the hope that any combining process would be extensively successful. The attempt, in the present condition of things, would probably result in the creation of a new sect. We all need a much larger measure of the Divine Influence to remove our prejudices, to clarify our spiritual vision, to impregnate our minds with the love of pure truth, to assimilate us more completely to the great Magnet of the universe — the Crucified One. When these results are accomplished in us, — and accomplished they may be, and should be, — then shall we be prepared for union, and then, doubtless, we shall be more attractive as well as more attracted than we now are.

Many other reasons might be suggested why we should cultivate a higher degree of personal holiness; but my present object confines me to this one point — the indispensableness of an advanced state of piety to the promotion of true Christian union. We are deficient in that "godliness" which "is profitable unto all things," and therefore profitable to the harmonizing of separated and alienated brethren. We have devoted much to the outward of Christianity; let us turn our care to the inward, and give more to the culture of piety and holy living by faith on the Son of God. Let us endeavor, by all the helps of Divine grace, to kill out more effectually the selfishness of our natures, and cultivate a supreme regard for the glory of Christ. Happy would it be for us and for others, would we but strive, "according to the power that worketh in us," to be more Christ-like, to be "crucified with Christ," to be "made conformable to his death," to be "sanctified wholly," to have our "whole body and soul and spirit preserved blameless," to be "filled with the Spirit," and so to follow the Saviour as that we "shall not walk in darkness, but have the light of life." The end to be sought is of incalculable importance. As a means for its attainment, our greatly increased sanctification is indispensable. The perfection of Christian union depends upon perfection of Christian character. For holiness, then, we should individually, unanimously, vigorously strive; and as we press on towards higher and still higher attainments, let us avail ourselves of the fulness of provision in the Dispensation of

Grace, which is preëminently the Dispensation of the Spirit.

3. WE MAY ILLUSTRATE, BY OUR OWN PRACTICE, THE GREAT PRINCIPLE, THAT THE WORD OF GOD IS THE SOLE AUTHORIZED STANDARD IN ALL MATTERS OF RELIGION.

The falsities of the Roman Antichrist may be generalized under three heads.

1. That a knowledge of religious truth and duty is to be derived, not exclusively from the Sacred Scriptures, but also and largely from other sources, as tradition, the writings of the Fathers, the opinions of the prelates, and especially of the Pope, and the adjudications of Councils. *Vox Ecclesiæ vox Dei*, is the idea, to repudiate which is fatal heresy. The Church, that is, the hierarchy, is not only the interpreter of God's communications, but is also the authorized teacher of much that God has left otherwise unrevealed. The Bible, thus interpreted, is only one source of religious knowledge, and is not of itself sufficient to direct a sinner in the way of salvation.

2. That the righteousness of Christ received by faith is not the sole ground of a sinner's acceptance with God; but that other things are to be recognized as meritorious causes of eternal life;

among which are, a particular relation to the Church of Rome; various ceremonial observances, such as fasts, penances, pilgrimages, invocations of the saints and the Virgin, confessions, masses, pecuniary contributions; and especially the superabundant holiness of the saints deposited in the Church, as a treasure, to supply the deficiency of Christ's merits, and subject to the disposal of the Pope and his authorized subordinates.

3. That the regeneration of a sinner is not effected entirely by the agency of the Holy Spirit, or even by the Spirit and the Word combined, but in part, if not mainly, by the influence of certain prescribed ceremonies which are represented as indispensable, not only as the mediums of the Divine Influence, but also as possessing in themselves a saving efficiency.

It was against these three falsehoods, in particular, so fatally subversive of the whole Christian system, that the partially enlightened and bold Reformers of the sixteenth century vehemently protested, and from whose baneful influence they vigorously endeavored to disenthral not only themselves, but their deluded contemporaries. Hence, they brought out prominently the three great principles of immortal Truth:

THE BIBLE, *the only authoritative source of religious knowledge.*

The Righteousness of Christ, *received by faith, the only ground of a sinner's justification before God.*

The Holy Spirit, *the all-sufficient Agent in the production of spiritual life in the soul of man.*

This trinity of propositions they held up to the wondering nations, and faithful history informs us of the power which God gave them in the emancipation of enslaved millions.

The effort to restore the Bible to its proper place in human estimation, was the result of a clear conviction that this Volume, the Gift of God, teaches all we need to know and to do in the department of Religion. The writings of the Reformers, though marred by some errors, abound with propositions and explanations which show conclusively how correct was their general theory; and in their zealous, self-denying, and often perilous endeavors to supply the people, in their own tongues, with the whole Book of God, we find their practice happily consistent with their theory. And from their day to ours, the tongues and the pens of Protestant Christians have repeated and multiplied the declarations of those giants of Reform; and, during the last half century, numerous Bible associations have practically demonstrated that the principles avowed are not the rhapsodies of sentiment, but the deliberate convictions of the understanding and the warm attestations of the heart. Who, of Protestant proclivities, has not admired, and quoted with his own endorsement, that terse, expressive proposition of the learned Chillingworth: "The Bible, the Bible, I say, the Bible only is the religion of Protestants?" And well did he add in the next sentence: "Whatsoever else they may believe as a matter of faith and religion, they cannot do it with coherence to their own grounds, nor require the belief of it in others, without most high and most schismatical presumption."

Yet, strong as have been the declarations of all Protestants upon this subject, and much as they have contributed towards the translation and distribution of the Bible, it may be a question if Protestants, of all denominations, have not more or less violated the great Principle which they have so often and so eloquently advocated. Luther said that "every man is born with a Pope in his heart." The errors of the papacy seem to be indigenous to human nature; and it would not be remarkable, if the best of men, partially sanctified, should betray the presence of some remnants of the old leaven. But how stands the fact? Do Protestants confine themselves to the Word of God as their sole instructor in religious truth and duty?[1] One of the most able and fascinating writers of modern times has drawn a beautiful word-picture in the following form: "All the doctors, Greek, Latin, French, Swiss, German, English, American, placed in the presence of the Word of God, are, altogether, only disciples who are receiving instruction. Men of the first times, men of the last, we are all alike upon the benches of the Divine School; and in the chair of instruction, around which we are humbly assembled, nothing appears, nothing elevates itself but the infallible Word of God. I perceive in that vast

1 The Reformation in Germany turned entirely upon this principle: "The Fathers must be tried by the Scriptures, and not the Scriptures by the Fathers." Then, when Luther, aided by Melancthon, had made the Bible common by his translation, and announced the clearness and certainty of its truths, without the aid of commentators; then it was that the errors of Popery, one by one, lost their hold upon the minds of the people, and a oneness of sentiment and faith was given to the whole body of reformers and their disciples everywhere, that vibrated at all points of Christendom, and put a newness of face on the kingdom of Christ. We, even in these days, have in some measure degenerated from the sacred oracles. We have had recourse to waters, collected from the living fountain, only in the receptacles in which human authors have deposited them, and where they are impregnated with the qualities of the fallible and fallen minds that have distributed them. We must drink these waters in greater purity, by retracing our steps to their source.—*Dr. Liefchild.*

auditory, Calvin, Luther, Cranmer, Augustine, Chrysostom, Athanasius, Cyprian, by the side of our cotemporaries."[1] If this be taken as a representation of what should be, it is more than beautiful, — the conception is sublime. If I am desired to regard it as descriptive of actual fact, I pause and consider. Passing over the "men of the first times" as the lights of a period long anterior to the Reformation, and even to the general triumph of the papacy "whose coming was after the working of Satan, with all power and signs and lying wonders," I would respectfully inquire if the "men of the last times," commencing with Martin Luther and ending with whom you please, have practically carried out in their formularies of doctrine and practice the boasted principle, "The Bible only the religion of Protestants?" It is no part of my purpose to detect and expose the inconsistencies and infirmities of others; I design merely to intimate that the loud proclamation and earnest advocacy of a great Truth is not always accompanied by a full submission to that Truth in its practical requirements; and that if this incongruity may be found in others, we may not take it for granted that we are wholly exempt from it ourselves.

[1] Puseyism Examined; by J. H. Merle d' Aubigné.

We are not strictly a Protestant denomination. We are, many of us, descendants of those brave men and women who protested against the abominations of Rome; but, as a Christian sect, we are not the offspring of the Reformation. Our name is nothing but a discriminative title, denoting at first but a single peculiarity, now standing for a class of ideas, and could easily be dismissed for the more comprehensive and original appellation, CHRISTIAN. But our principles are older than the papacy,—older than all the corruptions of ecclesiastical Catholicism. Along the ages there were a series of good men who maintained those principles, and protested against the perversion of evangelical Christianity and the schisms of the Christian Church; and to them we claim affinity. If it be asked where we were during the exciting and tumultuous scenes of the Reformation, I answer that, although few and feeble and scattered, we were there, not bearing indeed our present name, nor yet the name Anabaptist,[1] but advocating essentially our distinctive principles,

[1] No pains have been spared to trace our paternity to the Anabaptists of central Europe, a fanatical sect, of whom it has never been proved that they were immersionists. They repeated the rite, generally in the common form of the age, simply to render it valid; not as performed in a better mode, but by better hands.

and endeavoring to commend them to the reception of both the reformers and the reformed. Ever from the days of the Apostles we have professed to regard the Word of God as the only authentic source of religious knowledge, the sole arbiter of truth in all questions of religious faith and practice. The great Protestant sentiment upon this subject has always been ours; and neither Melancthon, nor Chillingworth, nor even the learned Professor at Geneva, ever constructed stronger utterances in its favor than have come from the lips and the pens of our brethren at all points along the line of our lengthened history. Our antiquity as a sect is of minor consequence; but we do attach value to the continuity of certain principles, commencing in the apostolic age, and running unbroken through the ages of papal error. We still avow the Bible to be the only authoritative Book of the Church, the only Rule of Christian faith and conduct, the Judge to whom in all religious questions our appeal is to be made, and whose decisions alone are ultimate and binding. Whoever may say, "To the Bible and Tradition," we are accustomed unanimously to say, "To the Law and to the Testimony," or, "To the Bible only."

After such statements, the inquiry may be started: "What more, my brother, do you desire?" Nothing more, certainly, by way of profession. The theory is "perfect and entire, wanting nothing." And is it not equally perfect in the spoken and the written professions of other evangelical denominations, whose practice, in some respects, we think, contradicts or ignores the principle? It may, therefore, be an unexpected, if not an unwelcome, question, if we do practically make the Bible our exclusive standard of truth and duty in religion. I ask not if our system of belief is concurrent with the teachings of the Sacred Scriptures; or, if the Christian ordinances, as administered by us, are essentially after the primitive pattern; or, if our ecclesiastical organizations are such as the Apostles, in our circumstances, would be likely to adopt; because these questions may, for the present, be answered in the affirmative, and yet the inquiry be legitimately urged, if we actually treat the Bible as we profess to regard it; if we do ourselves repair directly and exclusively to the Word of God for our religious knowledge; if our profession of the Christian faith, and our connection with a particular body of Christians are the results of our own investigations and intelligent convictions. Has tradition no authority with us? Has the education we received anterior to our conversion no influence in modifying our opinions and practices?

Are we never drawn into the Churches of which we are members by the power of example, of sympathy, of natural relationship, or of partiality to the "ministers by whom we believed," or by whose labors we are particularly edified? Has the Bible with us supreme authority, not only in theory but also in fact? Is it the Law of our hearts, our lips, our lives? Is it always the master, and never the servant, of our reason?

Perhaps no people are more accustomed than we to say to converts and to all inquirers after truth, "Go to the Scriptures. Read candidly and prayerfully, and there ascertain what you are to believe and what you are to practise." And yet, do we never depart from this most commendable advice by throwing in something else to incline inquirers in a desired direction? Do we trust them with the Bible only? Do we never interpose the influence of names, — the names of excellent men who thought and acted, as we think, rightly? We complain of others, and not without occasion, that they distribute tracts and books adapted to sectarian purposes. Do we never recommend and circulate human productions, as if something more than the Bible were necessary to lead perplexed minds to our conclusions? Of the numerous thousands who are every year identifying themselves with us by a Christian profession, how many can truly say that the Bible only is their Directory, — the lamp unto their feet and the light unto their path? What is the design, and what are the practical tendencies, of the "denominational literature" for the young and the old? Are our rising ministry never instructed in systems of divinity which others have prepared for their benefit? Those systems may be strictly scriptural; but do they who receive them always know by personal investigation that they embody the truth of God? And when they are supplied with "rules of interpretation," and told to apply them for themselves, are those rules not unfrequently such as are expected and intended to bring out certain results? Is Ecclesiastical History never made with us, as well as with others, to mould and modify our theological doctrines and our views of Church polity? Do we never, in a Summary of Faith, submit for examination a series of doctrinal propositions, or preceptive instructions, and recommend that they be compared with the Scriptures? And are not the points thus presented intended to be like the posts in a certain kind of fence, while the proof-texts to be culled from the Bible are, like flexile osiers, to be wattled in to complete the structure?

Have you never thought, my brother, of a peculiar fact in the history of theological institutions? The different sects have these "schools of the prophets," in all of which it is professed that a Biblical theology is taught. They certainly differ more or less in their instructions, else they might be consolidated, and, as I have shown, save expense, and make a better moral impression upon the community. They certainly train their candidates for the pulpit differently, and send them out for services that differ. Does not the spirit of sect rule largely in these institutions? If not; if the Bible is made the authoritative Guide, lead where it may; if the pupils are encouraged to make independent investigations, and taught to submit their reasons to the clearly ascertained will of God, — how shall we account for it that they so uniformly emerge as they entered, with no change but a confirmation of their preëxistent opinions, and firmer fixedness in their sectarian relations? And if the leaders are thus trained in a system, where the Bible is made to serve rather than rule, it cannot surprise us that the masses should follow their predilections, and seldom inquire "What saith the Lord?"

At the Council of Trent it is said that a copy of the Bible was placed upon an elevated throne, richly upholstered, in token of its supremacy. Yet the worthies there assembled proceeded to settle great questions of doctrine and polity without once referring to the Book thus nominally enthroned. Their action, if not designedly, was actually as bitter mockery of the inspired Volume, as was the conduct of another group, who put upon Christ a purple robe, and a reed in his hand! From that epoch, a new starting-point in the bloody march of spiritual despotism, the Bible ceased to be allowed even the appearance of supremacy, and its royal position was usurped by decrees and formularies of human manufacture. We lay the Bible upon our high places, both at home and in the house of worship, and treat it objectively with great outward respect; but do we really pay it all the reverence which these formalities would indicate? Does it hold the primary place as our Teacher of truth and duty?

We are constantly saying that if all Christians, with minds completely dispossessed of prejudice, and sincerely desirous to learn the divine will in order that they might do it, would devoutly repair to the Bible, and the Bible only, for information, they would not fail of their object; they would assuredly come into "the unity of the faith." And who can dispute the correctness of this assertion? Did not the Saviour say that if any man would

DO his Father's will he should KNOW the real truth? The Scriptures are not like the heathen oracles, equivocal or enigmatical, nor are they "of any private interpretation." If they were, how could they be "profitable for doctrine, for reproof, for correction, for instruction in righteousness?" They are a Revelation — an ἀποκάλυψις — of the will of God, containing the doctrines which he would have us believe, and the precepts which he would have us obey. He has informed us of the simple conditions upon which we may ascertain the meaning of this Paternal Gift, and these may be comprised under four heads:

That our motive in all be to glorify Him;
That we diligently search the Scriptures;
That we search them with childlike docility;
That we search with the spirit of obedience.

If all would follow his directions, they would learn his meaning, and therefore agree in their conclusions. To suppose it might be otherwise, would be to destroy confidence in the Scriptures, and impeach the wisdom, the veracity, and the goodness of their Divine Author.

But while such are the views that we proclaim, and that are not ours exclusively, we must not take it amiss if a question should be raised as to our consistency of practice. Do we examine the Word of God free from all prejudice or prepossession, entirely divested of the spirit of sect; and are our investigations prosecuted with that docile and obedient spirit, and with that purity of motive, which are indispensable to the certain discovery of the Divine will? If the Bible were now for the first time put into our hands as the one and only source of religious truth, are our minds in the proper attitude for the ascertainment of its true import? Are we sure that the conclusions to which we should come are identical with the propositions set forth in our present creeds, or summaries of faith and practice? Have we embraced these propositions because we first found them clearly taught in the Scriptures; or have we embraced them and committed ourselves to their defence, and afterwards looked for them, and found them the more easily in the Divine Word? I may be told that it matters very little how we came by our religious theory, provided we can prove it by the Scriptures. To such a pleader I respectfully reply, that unless he has, by personal investigation, made in the spirit of candor, with prayer for Divine illumination, and with honest practical intentions, derived his articles of belief directly from the Sacred Volume, he has no right to say that they are scriptural. He should know that almost anything may be "proved" by fragmentary citations from Scripture wrested from their connections, and that his proof-texts may, by a process of subornation, be false witnesses. Surely, there is a wide difference between hearing with docility what God says, and using his testimony to confirm what man says. Besides, he should not forget that in his treatment of the Scriptures, he is not such an one as God has promised to "guide in judgment," and to "teach his way." He has not only violated his own principle —"The Bible only is my religion"—but he has deviated widely from the Divine directions touching the discovery of truth, and therefore "the secret of the Lord" is not with him. He has not talked with Jesus by the way, and had the Scriptures opened to him by their heavenly Author; but he has embraced his system of theological theses, and then brought them to the inspired Word for corroboration. The Jews at Berea were "more noble" than this; they heard what Paul and Silas had to say, and were deeply interested in their interpretations and appeals; but they did not embrace the views presented, until they had carefully "searched the Scriptures daily whether those thing were so." Were I addressing him, instead of you, I would say: No, my brother; unless you have come unprejudiced, and free from all party bias, and with a truly humble, docile spirit, to the prayerful study of the Bible, you are not authorized to say that your system is scriptural. It may be so, because others before you may have fairly drawn it from the Fountain of living Truth; but you do not know it to be so, and all your selected proof-texts will never justify you in the use of very positive language respecting it. You have embraced the system without knowing it to be scriptural, and for other reasons than its Biblical verification; and, more than this, you have foreclosed the only avenue leading to that solid ground of certainty on which you might stand erect and challenge contradiction. Say not, then, that it is of little importance how you came into possession of your views, provided you can quote Scripture in their support. The question, Is the system yours? is legitimate and deserving of a considerate reply. A good title is of some importance in our religious as well as our secular affairs.

But the position thus assumed is indefensible in another respect. It practically undervalues the Word of God, and justifies the course of those denominations who resort occasionally to other sources of religious knowledge. They say, "The Bible, the Bible only," and yet in practice it is Tradition, or the Fathers, or Ecclesiastical History, or Articles, Homilies, Standards of Faith, Confessions, or something else in addition to the Bible.

We say, "The Bible, the Bible only," and yet, according to your theory, we may receive from some other source our theological principles, and employ the Bible merely for their confirmation and sanction. Thus perpetrating the very wrong which we profess to condemn, and which, perhaps boastfully, we allege that we avoid, our teachings are impaired in force by an inconsistent example.

The various plans of union which have been proposed and recommended have seemed to recognize the practicability of Christians coming together and being one without agreement in belief and practice. It may be presumptuous in me to express a doubt of the possibility of such an union; but the doubt is deeply fixed in my mind, and every new examination of the facts confirms it. I hear God inquiring, "Can two walk together except they be agreed?" and I understand the interrogation as involving a decided negative. If the fellowship of two, the smallest number, be impossible without agreement, I conclude that the same impossibility extends to a thousand or a million who may disagree. Any number of individuals can walk together *so far* as they are agreed, provided they consent to hold in abeyance the points respecting which they differ; but by a fixed law their real union cannot be stretched beyond the particulars in which they concur. I suppose that Christian union must have its basis in unanimity touching everything which the Scriptures make essential to Christian character and the Christian life. The union of the primitive Church was unquestionably of this kind. In matters pertaining to which they had no Divine instruction, they may have differed, nay, they did differ, and the Apostles advised them to be forbearing and charitable respecting those differences; but in all that Christ and his inspired servants taught them to believe and do, they were agreed and united. Theirs, therefore, was not merely an union of hearts, but also an union of minds. Their religious convictions were coincident; their religious practice was uniform. The word of God was to them supreme authority, and that word they interpreted alike.

One of the modes, then, by which we may promote that union among God's children which we acknowledge to be desirable, is to promote agreement among them with respect to Christian truth and duty. And this may be done by encouraging, in every practicable way, the careful, candid, devout study of the Scriptures as the one source of religious knowledge. How can we so effectively influence others to adopt this course, as by presenting in our own conduct the true example? THE WORD OF GOD ONLY: be that our motto, "known and read of all men." And let our action be faithfully suited to the sentiment: "The Word of God only, with no human addition; the Divine Revelation, clear, limpid, pure, just as it came from the heart of infinite Wisdom, Goodness and Truth. Turning away from man and all his utterances, let us apply our ear attentively, exclusively to the Divine Testimony. "I will hear what God the Lord will speak." And while we show definitively to all observers that we count as an outrage, and even as impiety, the attempt to put anything by the side of his Word, let us not fail to show also, and with equal definitiveness, that we are sincerely desirous to be enlightened and governed by that Word. Let us ever with true meekness and docility occupy "the benches of that divine School," where "nothing appears, nothing elevates itself in the chair of instruction, but the infallible Word of God." And when converts are multiplied around us, let us faithfully insist that they take their places in the same school as disciples of the Great Teacher. Let us not introduce them into the Church, and fasten upon them a sectarian name, and pledge them to the defence of a sectarian creed and the support of a sectarian policy, and afterwards direct them to the Bible as the Book from which they are to learn their Master's will. The Bible First, the Bible Always: be that our lesson, verbally taught, practically exemplified.

In this way we may contribute to Christian harmony. We shall thus take an important step towards the qualification of ourselves as a constituent portion of the great united whole. We shall become practically and really, what very many are now only theoretically and apparently, the disciples of Him who said, "Learn of me." We shall occupy ground upon which, if all come, all will agree, and upon which, if there be in all the proper moral feelings, there will assuredly be the union for which the Saviour prayed.

An incidental effect of such study of the Divine Word, and further contributive to the general result, is the spirit that will be nurtured in our own bosoms, — a spirit as far removed from the schismatical as is the spirit of heaven. A man who has adopted his theological principles, and arranged his system of religious ethics, and then comes to the Bible merely to corroborate and sanctify his preconceptions, pursues a course that will be likely to strengthen all his tendencies to separation and exclusiveness. He will be more of the controvertist than the peace-maker; more of the sectarian than the Christian. But the man who reverences the Word of God as supreme in excellence and authority; who comes to it, emptied of all human notions, and communes with it, sincerely desirous to be made wiser and better; who opens his soul fully to all the influences and impregnations of the truth, "as the truth is in Jesus," — will be sure, not only to learn how he may be saved, and what he must believe, and the duties he must practise, but also to imbibe a spirit that will render him more lovely in the eyes of both earth and heaven, and a more fit subject for that union which is yet to be realized, and for which high spiritual qualifications are indispensable. He lays his thirsting soul down to that "stream which makes glad the city of God," — the one stream of truth with which mingle no inflaming ingredients. He drinks in the spirit of the Bible, and it becomes incorporated with his moral being, and his spiritual improvement is obvious to all around him. It is seen that his feelings and disposition are formed after the New Testament model, and opponents of his views take knowledge of him that he has "been with Jesus," and learned of Him who is "meek and lowly in heart." Among the graces of his character are courtesy, gentleness, forbearance, condescension, kindness, simplicity, godly sincerity. He is "tender-hearted," "kindly-affectioned," and "follows after the things which make for peace, and things whereby one may edify another." The sermon on the mount he has heard with profit, for he is a living illustration of its practical excellence. The lesson of Jesus in the washing of his disciples' feet has not been lost upon him, for its spirit is wrought into his soul, and developed in his life. His visits to the Garden and the Cross have not been in vain; for he has there learned to endure suffering without a murmur, to be patient under goading provocations, to pray for his harshest tormentors, and to surrender all to the will of his Heavenly Father. How completely is his moral nature baptized into the spirit of the Bible; how thoroughly is he impregnated with its subduing, mellowing influence; how suitable a candidate is he for membership in that One Church which is a thing of the future!

4. WE MAY CHEERFULLY SURRENDER EVERYTHING ADVERSE TO UNION WHICH WE ARE NOT BOUND BY OUR ALLEGIANCE TO CHRIST TO RETAIN.

Under this head may be reckoned every sentiment or practice that cannot be shown to be scriptural; every feature in our general polity which we may know to be of human origin; everything that interferes with the healing process, and is not required of us by the Master. Surely, for the sake of such a good as the cordial union of the followers of Christ, we can afford to surrender whatever lies outside of the realm of prescribed duty.

"Yes," you say, and all say, "anything but Truth and Conscience." Let us, then, be candid and thorough in our investigations, and detect and repudiate whatsoever in us may unnecessarily hinder the reünion of a fractured, divided Church.

We do not, for we cannot, pretend to infallibility. Such an assumption we leave to the blinded papist, and to his foster son of the Oxford family, who welcomes the relation, and obsequiously

> . . . . "dextræ . . .
> Implicuit, sequiturque patrem non passibus æquis."

Dr. Oswald has said that "the possibility of error attends every mathematical demonstration." This possibility may be predicated of everything human; and Christians who are supposed to know their own weakness, their facility of aberration, and their exposure to misleading influences, are expected to be the last to claim exemption from this universal liability. We can afford to be the latest of the last to assume, either directly or by implication, that the whole truth, exclusive of all error, is assuredly with us. However willing we may be to submit our system to the most rigorous scrutiny, we lose nothing by the admission that there may be mistakes which we have overlooked. And however kindly we may think that we feel towards other denominations, and however charitably we may suppose that we carry ourselves towards them, it is quite possible that in these respects there may be some things not conformable to the divine standard.

Those who are under the influence of the sectarian spirit are unwilling to examine their religious scheme. They are committed to its support, and their humility is not equal to the trial that would ensue upon the discovery of an error, which, knowing it to be such, they could not honestly retain. But what is the benefit of a retention of error? Truth only can make us holier, happier, more useful. It is for our interest to discover and renounce whatever is unscriptural, and we should be grateful to any being, Divine or human, who might assist us in the purifying process. If ours be certainly "the faith once delivered to the saints," then may we "earnestly contend" for it against all encroachments; but, as there is a possibility that it may, at some points, be either more or less erroneous, it is surely befitting that our zeal should be tempered with carefulness and modesty. The main stream may have issued absolutely pure from the Fountain of Truth; but rivulets from other fountains are constantly seeking to become its tributaries, and that man knows little of the history of doctrinal theology and of Christian morals, and little of the insinuating power of error, who apprehends no danger of the infiltration of foreign mixtures. God has, in his goodness to man, kept the Bible pure. Happy, indeed, if we can preserve in their purity the living waters as they flow in the channels that man has excavated. Hardly here can we be too vigilant, too faithful.

If challenged to designate any particular in our system which is unscriptural and at the same time an obstacle to the desirable union of Christians, I reply that such a service would be alien to my design. I simply commend to others what I propose to myself—self-censorship. If we rigorously examine ourselves, and the whole ground we occupy, and thoroughly repudiate whatsoever is truly objectionable, we take an important step towards the contemplated result. "For if we would judge ourselves, we should not be judged." I request no brother to surrender any part of the gospel, be it either doctrine or precept; no, not even for the sake of peace; and were I to propose a measure involving such a result, his allegiance to the Saviour should prompt him to rebuke me for the unworthy suggestion. In making Christian union the altar upon which he is invited to lay a sacrifice, I ask not that Christian truth may be the victim, or that he may be the officiating priest. But I do entreat him, as I would charge myself before God, to examine with candor, and see if there be nothing about us that is extra-evangelical, and that we can spare in perfect consistency with all our relations to Zion's King and Zion's cause. Whatever denominational pride may suggest to the contrary, let us heed rather the impulses of Christian love, and scrupulously put far away every such element of evil. We constitute, in this country, one of the largest portions of Christ's visible Body. Let us renounce everything that disqualifies us for a happy reünion of the dismembered parts, and be not the last, but the first, to take our place in the line of Truth and Holiness, awaiting with prayerful hope the hour when the world shall again have a manifestation of real Christian Brotherhood.

5. WE MAY CAREFULLY REFRAIN FROM EVERYTHING THAT MAY UNNECESSARILY TEND TO WIDEN THE BREACH AMONG CHRISTIANS, OR TEND TO PERPETUATE ITS CONTINUANCE.

One objectionable feature in all the plans for Christian union which I have examined, is the apparent confidence with which certain positions are assumed as true which are really points in debate. There is too much of what logicians call *petitio principii*—the taking for granted of a fundamental proposition which remains to be proved. Were I to propose a plan, I might perpetrate the same mistake, and demand of others that they concur with me touching some points in relation to which they have serious, conscientious difficulties. Hence the purpose with which I commenced, to abstain from the exhibition of a formal plan, and confine myself mainly to suggestions that presuppose ourselves as well as others to be unprepared for the consideration of any such plan. There cannot be union until there shall be agreement, assimilation, and mutual attraction. We must all be deeply imbued with the spirit of Christ, and conformed in principle and practice to the Bible standard of Christian character; then may we unite and cohere with a fair prospect that our union will be permanent. But never can the desired result be approached by any attempt that involves this offensive begging of the question, a course of conduct that generally aggravates the original difficulty.[1] We

[1] The treatise of the late Dr. Harris, of England, entitled "Christian Union: or the Divided Church made One," a work of great ability, and commendable spirit, is unhappily disfigured by several of these unwarrantable assumptions. Vide Boston ed., pp. 85, 86, 110, 122, etc.

feel ourselves repelled by a proposition to unite upon terms that require us to renounce what we consider, and are known to consider, as gospel truth or gospel duty. We say, if we speak at all, that "We desire union as much as any class of Christians upon earth, and are willing to make any sacrifice for the object which we think our Master will approve; but you must not ask us to do violence to our convictions, deliberately acquired and honestly maintained." Occupying this dignified and defensible position, we should remember that others may be as conscientious and as sensitive as ourselves, and that any proposition for union coming from us that involves a sacrifice of principles which they regard as important, is likely to receive the answer which we have so firmly and properly given. He who would promote good feeling, and draw more closely the bonds of fraternal confidence, and open most widely the avenues to conviction, must cautiously abstain from all trespass upon the domain of Christian consciences. "Come over to us, and we will be one," may seem to be a very simple and easy mode of adjusting the whole matter; but wherever it is attempted, the probability of success is by the very act diminished. "Come, brethren in the Lord, let us examine the whole subject of our agreements and our differences, and let us pray together for light and grace," would be a far more courteous proposition, and a more likely mode of reüniting and healing the broken ligaments.

Other denominations have sometimes spoken of us with severity as uncharitable, bigoted, exclusive. May not some of this have been provoked by the manner in which we have spoken of them? The question is not gratuitous, and should lead to inquiry. We are accustomed, I believe, to attribute their bitter utterances to other causes more nearly connected with our distinctive belief and practice; but let us candidly inquire if some of the responsibility may not belong to ourselves, and if at this point there may not be gain both to ourselves and to the cause of God by greater carefulness. Where there is error, show it; where there is wrong reprove it; "considering thyself lest thou also be tempted." But let us abstain from the use of harsh judgments and reproachful epithets, which only irritate and provoke retaliation. It would seem as if some men — Christians they are called — had "no greater joy" than to see how their opponents will smart and writhe under their stinging sarcasms. Surely, their only motive for the discharge of such barbed missiles must be self-gratification; for they are not capable of supposing that any real good to others, or any glory to God, can result from this conduct. Are the wounded convinced of error, or more inclined to embrace the views of such assailants? Is any truth developed or recommended by this process? Is the Saviour pleased with such acts, or such a spirit? And who are these wounded ones? Are they not the disciples of Jesus? And is it not possible that through them the envenomed points have reached and pierced the Master of us all?

If we desire to convert to our views others whom we regard as in error, but little knowledge of human nature is requisite to show us that our truly politic course is to avoid everything like sneer, ridicule, or denunciation. "A brother offended is harder to be won than a strong city." Their views may be unscriptural and of pernicious tendency; but what is the most effectual mode of soliciting attention to these facts, and producing in their minds the conviction that shall lead to the desired changes? Every man can instantly decide upon the expedient course, which here is the right course, by one honest inquiry of his own heart. By omitting all that can give unnecessary pain, and adopting the language, tone, and manner of true Christian kindness, we conciliate, attract, and endear. I may be told that others are often the aggressors, and that we are only showing a becoming resentment, paying them in their own coin. Indeed! and have we forgotten what the Saviour says of retaliation, of non-resistance, of forgiveness, of "forbearing one another in love," of the charity that "is not easily provoked" but "endureth all things?" "Becoming resentment!" What words are these from lips that monthly or bi-monthly press the cup of communion, and that were taught in early life to lisp the Lord's prayer! Have we yet to learn the lesson, "Be not overcome of evil, but overcome evil with good?" The reflex influence of kind words and acts upon our own hearts is softening and soothing; upon the hearts of others, subduing and melting; and such hearts soon clasp and throb in unison. Call a brother an opponent, and treat him as such, and, whatever he was, unless he has a large measure of the spirit of Christ, he becomes an opponent, and places himself in an attitude of resistance, if not of defiance. But, allow him the name by which he chooses to be called; concede to him the right of private judgment; attribute to him no motives which he disavows; assume no airs of superiority, but approach him as an equal; respect the delicacy of his conscience, and reason with him in the spirit of fraternal gentleness and affection, — and he is surely one of that small class of the intractable and irreclaimable, if he does not reciprocate your spirit, and welcome with gratitude the very impressions which you would fain leave upon his mind.

Much of that feeling among Christians which passes by the sacred name of Charity, is little else than masked disaffection, and, stripped of its disguise, would be denominated hypocrisy. What Leighton says of Humility, that he never heard it discoursed upon in an humble manner, is quite as true of this much-abused, dishonored Charity, which is often the most misrepresented in spirit by those who commend it most in word; it is explained and recommended in a most uncharitable way. You, my brother, I venture to say, have read many a book, and heard many a sermon, and listened to many a conversation upon Charity that exposed a painful deficiency of the lovely grace. The uncharitable — that is, all such as do not agree with the writer or the speaker — are considered as fair game, and every now and then there is a cut or a thrust which somebody must feel to the heart's centre. Alas! how imperfect we are! How often we are the victims of self-deception! Here is a point of special danger where we need to set a double guard. Malignity, hidden behind a Christian grace, shoots envenomed arrows, and injury is done which brings that grace into disrepute. Unless our Charity is genuine, let us not talk of it. If it be genuine, it needs no talk. It is eminently a practical grace, and shows itself sufficiently in tone, temper, and action. They who have the most of it are generally the least aware of it themselves, and therefore never boast of it.

We all profess to deplore the schisms among Christians, and to desire that they may be healed; and yet, how often do we hear regrets and wishes upon this subject accompanied by expressions of the most schismatical tendency. It is too common to endeavor to fix on others the guilt of schism, and to represent ourselves as the innocent victims of the wrong. I well recollect an instance in which a considerable number of Christians of different denominations agreed to meet once a month on the broad basis of their "maximum of agreement," and pray and labor jointly for the advancement of religion in the place of their residence. They desired, they said, to draw more closely the bonds of Christian fellowship, and show to the world that, in the main, they were agreed and united. At the first meeting remarks were made by the presiding clergyman with respect to the origin of divisions among Christians, and the causes which prevent an entire and cordial union, that deeply wounded many present, and proved fatal to the whole project. What is the real value of an union, where each constituent denomination says, "We are disposed to enter into the proposed combination, but we do it with the distinct understanding that we are right and you are wrong?"

You, my brother, have doubtless admired those beautiful and affecting words which Milton represents Adam as addressing to Eve, after they had wearied themselves and wounded each other with mutual complaints and recriminations:

> "But, rise; let us no more contend, nor blame
> Each other, blamed enough elsewhere; but strive,
> In offices of love, how we may lighten
> Each other's burden in our share of woe.'

And you have admired still more the address of Abraham to his kinsman, Lot, — an address which has acquired for him the designation of "The first gentleman," as for other reasons he is called "The Father of the Faithful:"—"Let there be no strife, I pray thee, between me and thee, and between my herdmen and thy herdmen; for we are brethren." Investigation might have led to a discovery of the original offender, and the true guilt of each party might have been ascertained. But *cui bono?* Where would have been the advantage of such a result? Justice might have been administered, but alienation and animosity would have been deepened and perpetuated. "Where lies the responsibility?" is, I admit, a question of some importance; but is it not far better, if we sincerely desire the restoration of harmony, for every party to confine the inquiry to itself, and thus avoid everything like crimination and reproach?

Controversy may sometimes be unavoidable, and, within certain limits, and governed by certain rules, it may be useful. It has been said to be "the wind by which truth is winnowed," and also that, by the collision of mind with mind in the process, "the sparks of truth are elicited." But the history of sixteen centuries will show conclusively that whatever may be its advantages in other departments, its utility in the Christian Church is extremely limited. Strange as it may seem, yet honesty requires the admission, that religious controversies have often been distinguished by peculiar acrimony and bitterness. Who does not know that even now they inflict wounds that fester long and deeply, and heal slowly and imperfectly? Who has not witnessed the exasperation of feeling produced by a single tract or pamphlet, not by the clearness or cogency of its arguments, but by the rasping character of its hints and surmises, implications and caricatures? Mischief is sometimes done by a newspaper paragraph of twenty lines, that cannot in a whole generation be repaired.

It is a delightful fact that controversy among the evangelical denominations has of late years assumed a milder form, and therefore produces less of inflammation. Its spirit has become subdued, and far more candid, as if brethren were dealing not with carnivorous antagonists, but with brethren, the children of one Father. Certainly, on our own side, we have occasion to be grateful that the discussion of one class of disputed subjects has fallen into the hands of such men as Baldwin, Chapin, Judson, Ripley, Jewett, Hague and Curtis. Of their argumentation I say nothing; of the temper exhibited in their productions I might speak in terms of the highest commendation. And upon all questions, whether of Christian doctrine or of ecclesiastical polity, the spirit of controversy has undergone a favorable modification. Misrepresentation and wholesale abuse are not so common as formerly, and Christians can oppose one another's principles and practices with less of personality, and less of unjust, gratuitous insinuation. "Her Ladyship of Babylon" is not so frequently named as the foster-mother of all denominations but one, and reproachful epithets are current at less value than in the days of our fathers. God grant that these improvements may proceed, and that the time may speedily come when everything unnecessarily vexatious and irritating shall be discarded, and when all comparisons of opinions and all discussions of differences shall be conducted in the gentle and generous spirit of the gospel. How comprehensive and yet how definite that phrase from an Apostle's pen, specifically translated, "Speaking the truth in love" — *ἀληθεύοντες ἐν ἀγάπῃ*, — truthing in love, — being, thinking, feeling, speaking, acting affectionately true, at all times, in all places, towards all persons!

Is it not possible that we may sometimes, with wrong intentions, or in a wrong spirit, remind others how unkindly their ancestors treated our fathers? History certainly tells some exciting tales upon this subject; but is it profitable to ourselves, or to the cause of God, to remember them, and to use them either for attack or defence in denominational controversy? Those who perpetrated the foul wrongs, like the victims of their severity, have all gone to a world where wrong is equitably rectified, and right satisfactorily vindicated. The successors of those persecutors are no more the inheritors of their guilt, than we are partakers of the sufferings of our abused predecessors. Let us rejoice that a change has come over the once oppressive and persecuting sects; and, so long as they exhibit not the spirit, and justify not the misdeeds, of their fathers, let us not taunt them with their ecclesiastical lineage, or hold them responsible for wrongs in which they did not participate, and in the condemnation of which they may be as sincere as ourselves.

We are every year receiving into our Churches ministers and private members who have seen occasion, as the result of new views, to change their ecclesiastical relations by embracing our principles and adopting our distinctive practice. It is very natural for us to be pleased when such changes occur, and to refer to them as corroborative proof of the correctness of our system. Surely, it is said, if the evidence did not preponderate very much in our favor, such persons would not have yielded to it all their prejudices of education, or sacrificed so freely their social interest, or exposed themselves to so much obloquy from their former associates. But, in proclaiming the facts, is it necessary to speak as if signal victories had been gained? From the prominence given to such cases, the inference is drawn that more importance is attached to acquisitions of this kind than to conversions from the world. The ordinary effect of such boasting is irritation of feeling and provocation to a more embittered resistance, if not to reprisals. Just in proportion as we magnify the value of such converts, will others be likely to detract from their worth, and hold them up to the world as losses of minor consequence. In disputes about loss and gain, the warfare is likely to become personal, damaging the reputation and diminishing the future influence of the seceders; or, if character escape unscathed, they are liable, under such a goading process, to be driven to an extreme, and to become the most fierce and intolerant of all sectarians. "He that departeth from evil maketh himself a prey." But, whatever the effect upon the individuals concerned, the almost certain result is an aggravation of party spirit. The breach that separates Christians, like the fosse in military fortifications, is made broader and deeper and more impassable than ever; and the very bridge over which these brethren passed in their transition is hewn away, and the probability of further conversions is greatly diminished. How much more Christian-like, and how much more pacific in its tendencies, would be our conduct, if in such cases we should carefully abstain from everything like exultation or triumph! How much more certain might we be of the approving smile of our Lord; how much more conservative and healing would be our influence on his riven, bleeding Body! By pursuing this prudent and conciliatory course, I see not that we yield anything of principle, or that we compromise any interest of our adorable Master. On the contrary, we should, I cannot doubt, subserve the best interests of that kingdom which is not of this world, and which needs not the spirit of this world for its advancement. I plead for nothing cowardly or craven-hearted. Let us not flinch from the manly defence and the wide-spread propagation of the whole truth as we derive it from the Word of God. Let us pour abroad the whole current of our moral power in order to bring all men to "the knowledge of the truth," and to "the obedience of Christ;" and then, if other Christians fall in with us, singly or in groups, we may certainly be both pleased and grateful. But let us, as followers of Him who studied more to soothe than to irritate, more to persuade and allure than to provoke and repel, be cautious as to the language we employ, the measures we adopt, and the spirit we exhibit. Let the victories, great or small, which the truth achieves, all go to grace, not our triumph, but the Saviour's.

Learned men of other denominations have made extraordinary concessions touching our interpretation of certain Greek terms in the New Testament, as also with respect to the conformity of our peculiar practice to the meaning of those terms, and to apostolic and ancient usage. These concessions are certainly of some value in argument; but it may fairly be questioned if we have not sometimes employed them disingenuously, and in a way more fitted to offend than to convince. It is hardly honorable to select detached sentences, or fragments of sentences, and so remove them from their connections as to make them express more, or less, or something else, than the author intended to convey. Some writers have complained of our injustice in this particular; and it is not improbable that hereafter, in their attempts to avoid the possibility of misrepresentation, authors may be less candid.

We are accustomed to speak freely, perhaps sometimes complacently, of our great and rapidly increasing numbers; and we not unfrequently do it in such relations and in such a manner as to indicate that hundreds of thousands are a very strong argument. Once we were few and feeble, and claimed to be regarded as the "little flock" to whom was promised the kingdom. Now, we are so large a people, and annually increasing by such numerous additions, that surely the Lord must be on our side, and we must be his special favorites.

We have indeed an immense number of communicants, and it would be occasion for joy could we see that they are distinguished for personal godliness, for a high order of religious culture, for united vigorous efforts to evangelize the world. Considering well the real facts, have we not occasion for humility and solicitude? It is a very serious question if our numerical strength is not likely to prove our moral weakness, and, consequently, if our anticipations of a glorious future should not be moderate. Why, then, should we, by such frequent reference to growing numbers, minister nutriment to denominational pride, and institute comparisons adapted, if not intended, to mortify other sects, by reminding them of their numerical inferiority? Bad passions are stimulated on both sides, and obstacles to a greater Christian fraternity are multiplied.

Pointed arguments to incite our Churches to benevolent activity are often derived from sectarian sources. "Other denominations are active, and, unless we move with greater speed and energy, will take the ground." "Other denominations are supplying the destitute with ministers, and schools, and books, and, unless we bestir ourselves, we shall be left far in the rear." Such motives we hear urged, and often with greater earnestness than the higher considerations, — the command of Christ, the value of souls, the obligations of humanity. These appeals may not harm other denominations, except, perhaps, by goading them on to additional efforts for the lengthening of their own sectarian cords, and the strengthening of their sectarian stakes. But their influence upon our own people is not of the most healthful kind. They learn to regard others as our competitors for territory, and to consider as lost every acquisition which others may make, or may prevent us from making. They learn to look upon the religious enterprises of the different sects as struggles for precedence, — as the means of extending and strengthening party influence; and their contributions are liable to be made, not so much for the advancement of Christ's kingdom, or the salvation of souls, as for the pushing forward of denominational aggressions, and the preoccupancy of coveted territory. The moral bearing of such appeals to the spirit of sect can easily be apprehended. The effect must ever be such as the lovers of true benevolence and Christian harmony will deplore. How much better, in all respects, would it be to say: "Come, brethren in the Lord, redeemed by precious blood, let us consider our duty to Christ and to perishing men, and enter vigorously upon its faithful performance.

Our brethren of other denominations are in the field, and laboring with commendable zeal and encouraging success. God honors their efforts with his Spirit's blessing, and they are doing an immense amount of good. Let us gird ourselves for the service, and go forth where others have not gone, and endeavor to do the work assigned us by our Master. Time is short, and our period of labor is hastening to its conclusion. Sinners all over the world are dying and passing away to the retributions of eternity. Let us not linger. Constrained by love to Christ and love to souls, let us act with promptness and energy, and endeavor, before we go to our final account, to do something for the salvation of men and the glory of our Redeemer."[1]

"The Jews have no dealings with the Samaritans." This brief statement reveals much respecting not only the spirit that prevailed in those parties, but also the means by which that spirit was kept alive and active. In their secular, as

1 Andrew Fuller travelled much in England and Scotland on behalf of the Serampore Mission. It is said that he took the largest collections when he preached on the love of Christ, and made no reference to any lower class of motives. He bore to the treasury many a liberal gift from persons of various denominations.

well as their spiritual affairs, they avoided all intercourse. They were shy of each other's society, and studiously refrained from everything that might soften the asperity of their hatred, and lead to some reciprocity of kind offices. Thus was the breach between them widened year by year, and Gerizim and Jerusalem became more and more the rallying points of hated and hating partisans. And have you not, my brother, witnessed a propensity among religious sects to confine their social intercourse and their secular patronage within sectarian limits? Have you not seen men in every line of business expecting and receiving the preference, solely on denominational grounds? And have you not seen the effect of all this upon Christian character, contracting the heart, narrowing the circle in which the sympathies play, and giving to the whole moral being an aspect of illiberality and exclusiveness altogether unlovely? I submit the question, if to counteract these anti-social tendencies of the spirit of sect, we ought not to take special pains to bring Christians of different denominations more together, and to secure more of that familiar acquaintance which we all believe would produce favorable results? And should we not render good service to the Christian cause by regarding less than we do, in the distribution of our social attentions and our secular patronage, the influence of sectarian considerations? The law of brotherly love may justify many preferences; but the danger lies in the limitation of our brotherly love within too small a circle. It is bad enough that the lines of division are so distinct in our ecclesiastical organizations. Why should these lines run through social and commercial life, and keep Christians of different names from coming in contact at any point? Is there nowhere upon earth an unexceptionable place where those who may warrantably hope to meet in heaven, may come together, and look one another in the face, and read in one another's character the lineaments of a holy relationship?

6. WE MAY COÖPERATE WITH ALL CHRISTIANS IN EVERYTHING NOT INTERDICTED BY THE LAWS OF CHRIST.

The laws by which our conduct, as citizens of Zion, is to be governed, we ascertain, not from our covenant engagements to any particular Church, not from any usages of our denomination, not from any Declaration or Confession drawn up by men, however wise or holy, — but from the Word of God, candidly and prayerfully examined by ourselves. "There is one Lawgiver," the Lord

Jesus Christ, and he allows no one to stand between him and his subjects as the authoritative interpreter of his laws. The interpretations of neither the minister nor the Church are binding upon the membership. Christ, as Legislator and Judge, holds us individually and directly responsible, both for a right understanding of his laws, and for complete obedience to their requirements. Our allegiance to him is paramount to all other; and we have no right to enter into any association, or become subject to any authority, that will interfere with entire submission to his will as expressed in his inspired Word. No Church or combination of Churches, no minister or convention of ministers, not even "The Denomination,"—that great, indefinite abstraction,—has any prerogative in the department of conscience, either to make new laws for the regulation of our Christian conduct, or to suspend any law which Christ has given us. The statement that fell from his own lips is worthy of repetition: "One is your Master, even Christ, and all ye are brethren." By becoming acquainted with his will, we shall know how far we may proceed in any direction, and be able to determine, on all occasions, the prescribed boundaries within which our action must be faithfully confined. If we are desirous to know what, in any given case, we should do, Jesus says expressly to every one of us, as he did to the lawyer, "What is written in the Law? How readest thou?" He authorizes us to expect no new revelation, but ever remands us to the one we have. If we would ascertain the limits of our responsibility, and discover the line beyond which we must not go, even though prompted by the best of motives and treading in the steps of the best of men, we hear our Master saying, "Search the Scriptures, — they contain the statutes of my kingdom." If we would discover the spirit by which we should be governed in our intercourse with the Church and the world, this also is matter of Law, and every necessary direction will be found in the New Testament.

It is not for me to specify how far any one, beside myself, may go in his intercourse and coöperation with Christians of other sects; for this would be an invasion of the sacred domain of his conscience, an unwarrantable interposition of my private opinion between him and his spiritual Sovereign. I can determine for myself the extent and the limitations of my own duty, and no man or body of men, secular or religious, shall dictate to me my duty in this or any other department of Christian action. I shall make up my own estimate of the courtesies which I owe to the disciples of Jesus of every name, and shall pursue that course of conduct which accords with the laws of Christ as I understand them. This right I have surrendered to no denomination, no voluntary association, no Church. It is inherent and inalienable by virtue of my sonship in Christ; and it is the indefeasible right of every Christian disciple.

And yet I suppose I may, without assumption or immodesty, exhort my fellow-disciples to inquire carefully, and see if we cannot, consistently with our allegiance to the Son of God, and in ways that will be pleasing to him, exhibit towards other denominations more of the truly fraternal spirit than we have sometimes manifested, and make some additional advances towards that union which all the truly spiritual admit to be desirable. I ask them not, as I would not be myself asked, to transcend any scriptural limitations; but I surely may entreat them to examine anew, and decide for themselves if the friends of Christ cannot be more familiar with one another, more affectionate in their intercourse, more disposed to join their forces in efforts for the advancement of the common cause. It might not be wholly pertinent for me to inquire how Christ and his Apostles would act in this matter, were they to reäppear on the earth and be placed in our circumstances, for that is a point concerning which no one could give a better answer than his own opinion; and yet it is well often to propose the question, and to bring our minds, with such light as we have, to the formation of an opinion that may have some bearing upon our conduct. It is certainly better than to ask the advice of any sectarian in Christendom. But the true course, unquestionably, is to consult the teachings and the life of Christ, and the instructions and examples of his inspired Apostles, and thus, in the fear of God, and in full view of our responsibility to the Head of the Church, discover for ourselves individually the path of duty, and ever walk in it with all humility and firmness. If we enter upon this investigation divested of the spirit of sect, and resolved, as duty may seem to be indicated, to act, fearless of all denunciation, domestic or foreign, we may find that our views upon this subject have been too narrow, and our policy too restricted. I say not that there has been bigotry, for that is a word which ought to be sparingly used; but I cannot avoid the conviction that there has often been in ourselves, as well as in other sects, a spirit of exclusiveness quite uncalled for by the requirements of the gospel, and exceedingly pernicious in its effects upon both our Christian character and our Christian usefulness. It may be said that we are often provoked to it by the treatment we receive from others. Be it so, as matter of fact;

and thus we learn the tendency of exclusiveness to alienate and drive farther asunder the different sections of God's people; and thus, also, we see what must be the reäction upon others of our own exclusiveness. Why should we, even under provocation, pursue a course to which we find it painful to be provoked? And should we not exhibit more of the spirit of Christ, and set a better example, by patiently enduring the provocation, and steadily persisting in a kind, conciliatory course of conduct? Should we not more effectually subdue the wrong spirit in others, and win them over the more certainly to the path of fraternal concord, by forgiving than by resenting the injury? It seems to me that one of the primary lessons taught us in the New Testament, is the art of overcoming evil with good. There is a philosophy in the power of forgiveness and kindness worthy of our profoundest study. Who has ever availed himself of that power to its full extent? God accomplishes wonders by it, we ourselves being witnesses. Every reader of the Sacred volume must be aware of the special pains taken by Christ and his Apostles to show, both by precept and example, how much more can be effectuated by endurance than by resistance, by the "soft tongue" that "breaketh the bone" than by harsh retorts that madden the spirit. When shall we see the lessons upon meekness and gentleness which they have taught us fully exemplified? When shall we see a fair experiment of the efficacy of Christian patience and forbearance to dissolve the frost of sectarian prejudice, and promote the restoration of Christian fellowship?

But, says one, — and he possibly speaks for many, — "I cannot conscientiously associate in any religious relation with such a sect, lest I should countenance certain things in their system which I firmly believe to be wrong." He suggests an underlying principle of great importance. We certainly must not countenance wrong by act any more than by word. But the question now pertains to his application of the principle. It requires a nice discrimination to draw the line beyond which he may not proceed without countenancing what he ought to reprehend. And he may be rendered thoughtful by an inquiry with respect to his consistency. Is there nothing wrong in his own denomination, or in the Church where he holds his membership, which, if free association involves the offence, he is constantly countenancing? Where, in such a case, is his conscience? Does he not sustain religious relations to many, and openly co-operate with them in religious organizations, whom he knows to be derelict in Christian morals? Alas for the deceptions which we practise upon ourselves! How easy, where love is wanting, to find occasion for the stringent application of conscientious scruples! As in the Church we too often place opinions above piety, so in society we place them above morals; and while we shrink from social intercourse with persons who hold some errors, though of the most correct conduct, we do not hesitate to act in fraternal concert with professors of our own creed of very doubtful character. We do well not to countenance anything objectionable; but were we far more tolerant of opinions, and less tolerant of immoralities, we should exhibit much more of the spirit of the gospel.

The grave question, and one that involves great interests, is this: May we not go much farther than we do, in association with all the friends of Christ, without violating any law of the Master, without damage to any principle or practice that is properly dear to us, and without any harm to our personal godliness? If others show a disinclination to any such increase of familiarity and coöperation, and repel our generous approaches, then the responsibility of separation is theirs, and we shall have the delightful reflection that we have made a sincere movement, from which we anticipated healing results; and that by so doing we have endeavored to comply with the apostolic direction to "follow after the things which make for peace." But, allowing that our advances are repulsed, may we not hope that their repetition, in a Christian manner, and with much prayer for the Divine blessing, will be ultimately successful? Is not the issue sought of sufficient importance to justify persevering and long-continued effort?

There is certainly some common ground upon which all the regenerated can meet, and show to one another and to the world that there are some ligaments that remain unbroken. Let us ascertain that common ground, and be ever ready to occupy it on equal terms with all who love the Saviour. The exhortation of the Apostle to the Church at Philippi is exactly appropriate: "Whereto we have already attained, let us walk by the same rule, let us mind the same thing."[1] Here, it is assumed as a principle that agreement is the basis of union; it is taken for granted that on some points all Christians must agree; it is proposed that, as far as they do agree, they should cordially unite and coöperate; and it is more than intimated that by such a course they would most

[1] See an excellent Discourse from these words, entitled "The Principle of Christian Union," by Rev. William Hague, D. D. Boston: 1841.

effectually promote further coincidence of opinion. "If in anything ye be otherwise minded, God shall reveal even this unto you."[1] By walking harmoniously as far as we are agreed, we may rationally expect such additional illumination as will enable us to see other points alike, and thus to go on step by step until all differences shall disappear, and we find ourselves "one in Christ Jesus." The same Apostle expressed himself as painfully anxious for his brethren at Colosse, at Laodicea, and as many as had not seen his face in the flesh, "that their hearts might be comforted, being knit together in love, and unto all riches of the full assurance of understanding, to the acknowledgment of the mystery of God, and of the Father and of Christ;" thus plainly intimating that union of hearts would conduce to

[1] "Our testimony against error is surely far more exemplary and striking when we walk with our fellow-Christians as far as we are agreed, and leave them at the point where they diverge from the right path, than when we refuse to accompany them at all. By the former mode of conduct, we prove that, if we depart from any of the opinions or observances of our brethren, it is only at the irresistible voice of duty to God, and not from want of love towards *them;* while, by pursuing the ordinary course of sectarianism, we rather appear to disapprove of characters than of sentiments, and to contemn our fellow-Christians more than their errors." — *Mrs. Romeo Elton.*

the extension of their acquaintance with divine things, and, consequently, to a multiplication of the points of agreement. By the cultivation of kind feelings, and the exhibition of a liberal spirit, and the adoption of a generous course of action, we might hope, with aid from on high, to bring Christians more frequently and more closely together, that so they might familiarly compare their respective systems with the Word of God, and elevate the whole into entire conformity to that one perfect standard.

It deserves serious inquiry if great good might not result from the extension of our reading on a more liberal scale. An English writer, of much celebrity, says: "It would be a considerable help to the enlargedness of view and feeling, which this junction of the various religious bodies in our own country and in other parts calls for, were Christians to accustom themselves to read the works of writers of other religious denominations, as well as of their own; both those which detail their operations for the spread of the gospel, and which announce their particular views of Christianity in their own language. They would thus learn to give men credit for integrity and diligence in espousing opinions different from their own, whom they had previously imagined to be the slaves of prejudice, or victims of indolence. They would see that there were reasons for those opinions, which might easily determine the adoption of them by a certain class of minds, without any impeachment of their sincerity or piety. They would be gratified, too, by perceiving how much of truth and godliness had been established in the earth by the exertions of others not in conjunction with themselves, and hail as fellow-laborers those who, though they wrought in a different field, and after a different manner, were sowing the same seed of truth and righteousness, and reaping the same results as themselves, under the evident token of the Divine approbation and blessing." Our obligation to patronize a denominational literature cannot be paramount to our obligation to subserve the higher and broader interests of the Christian cause. Were it suitable, I might name religious newspapers published by other denominations in which our brethren would find immensely more than they may have expected to approve and admire. We might occasionally meet with an offensive paragraph; but, leaving it as an offset to some things equally objectionable on our own side, we should learn, and rejoice to learn, that other Christians are laboring for the promotion of truth and righteousness in the world, that they have at heart the good of souls and the glory of Christ, and that they have in large measure the Divine favor. Those publications advocate in the main the same great principles as our own; they exhibit essentially the same spirit; in ninety-nine parts of a hundred they contain nothing exceptionable, nothing that even sectarian optics can detect as contrary to the views which we entertain. It may be said that the courtesy which I recommend would not be reciprocated, and our effort would be practically useless. So we judge, *a priori*, and not, I am sure, as the result of experiment. Let the attempt be made in the true spirit of conciliation, and, if it fail, the world will see that we have done, in this direction, the friendly thing. This want of confidence in the utility of kind, pacific endeavors, and especially in the promise of Him who has appointed them as the means of overcoming evil, is the bane that paralyzes all effort for the restoration of harmony. And here is a point where Satan, the arch-divider of the Church, applies his perverse ingenuity. "It will do no good," he says, and we believe him. "Patronize exclusively your own publications," he adds, "and let others take care of theirs;" and we take his advice. The Saviour looks down, and repeats his own words, "All ye are brethren."

Several instances, like those of Douglas of Cavers, Jenkins of Assam, Wylie of Calcutta, Frye of Baltimore, Hill of Boston, and others, have occurred, where members of other communions have generously contributed to the aid of our Foreign Missions, and we have hailed them as indications of a truly liberal spirit. We love such donors, not for the sake of their gratuities, but because we perceive in them elements of character that raise them superior to all party distinctions, and bring them into fellowship with all who love and serve the Son of God. Were we to know that prominent individuals among us are annually or occasionally contributing to aid the benevolent activities of other denominations, should we consider them as manifesting the same lovely spirit, and entitled, for the same reasons, to a similar commendation? We should not, I suppose, deny their right to make such contributions; but would not many question the propriety of their conduct? It would be said of them, that they were diverting so much from the treasuries of their own societies, and that they were countenancing error and assisting in its propagation. But a careful analysis of all the feelings and principles involved in this double objection might reveal the presence of sectarian selfishness. When others make donations to our funds, they do it, not because they subscribe to all our views, but because they regard us as Christians engaged in a good work. What should hinder us from reciprocating the favor, and on the same broad basis? In patronizing the missionary efforts of any of the evangelical denominations, how much of error or of wrong should we countenance? Should we not, on the contrary, encourage a great amount of good? And, taking into the account every consideration, may we not believe that "with such sacrifices God" would be "well pleased?" If it be not inconsistent with our allegiance to Christ, then surely it is a service from which we need not be repelled by any apprehension suggested by sectarian casuistry. Were these acts of kindness and confidence more frequently interchanged by different denominations, the effect would be salutary upon themselves, and the impression upon the world would be more of that kind which we all regard as desirable. It is not the money benefit, but the moral advantage, for which I plead, — the multiplying and the strengthening of the connectives which unite the people of God. Take an illustrative fact. A lady in England, soliciting contributions for a Missionary Society in the town where she resided, called upon a pious tradesman who was not, like herself, of the Established Church. On entering, she said, "I wait on you, sir, from the Church Missionary

Society, because I have undertaken to call at every house in my division; but, as I believe you are not a Churchman, I cannot presume to calculate upon your subscription; and, though we are happy to receive support from any one, I ought not, perhaps, to expect it from you; and, therefore, having fulfilled my engagement by calling, I will now cheerfully take my leave." — "Stop, madam," said he; "I cannot suffer you to go away thus. It is true we have a Missionary Society of our own; but, when I consider how long I have lived in this place, and how little, comparatively, has been done here in a religious point of view until the formation of your society, I am truly thankful to God for his goodness, and you shall take the names of my wife and daughter, as humble but cheerful contributors." While he said this, "the springs which were in his head" — to use the quaint phraseology of John Bunyan — "did send the waters down his cheeks." The lady, after receiving the subscription of the Wesleyan, said, "Now, sir, as you have been so kind and liberal towards our Society, you must allow me to give you a testimony of my good-will towards yours." Accordingly, she insisted upon his accepting from her own purse a donation for the Wesleyan Missionary Society. "Truly," says Dr. Hague, after mentioning these facts, "when a charity so candid and reciprocal as this shall pervade the Church, divisions will be comparatively nominal and harmless; for, as the body without the spirit is dead, so sectarianism bereft of its selfish spirit is dead also."[1] To all this, from the pen and the heart of an esteemed brother, I cordially subscribe, with the wish that he may live to see sectarianism die of quick consumption, and to officiate at its interment. He will pronounce no eulogy upon the departed, and have none to comfort with the hope of a resurrection. The Devil and his angels will be the only mourners, and in mid-heaven will be heard the anthem, long since hushed, "GLORY TO GOD IN THE HIGHEST; AND ON EARTH PEACE, GOOD-WILL TOWARDS MEN."

Among the means that would contribute to the desired result, I must include especially prayer,—enlightened, earnest, universal prayer. Through Christ we all have "access by one Spirit unto the Father." We all believe in prayer as an instrument of wondrous power, not only in its reflex influence upon the character of the petitioner, but also in its mysterious effectiveness in securing blessings that God has to bestow. According to the Word of God, much is made dependent upon

[1] "Principle of Christian Union."

prayer, much is promised to prayer, much has been accomplished by prayer. United prayer is encouraged; and the assurance of success is given to the smallest number who shall agree in the service. In the very atmosphere of a prayer-room there is something that rebukes all selfishness, and pride, and strife, and intolerance, and every evil of imperfect humanity, and that stimulates and nurtures "whatsoever things are lovely and of good report." Christians who pray much together have their views harmonized and their feelings assimilated, and they become attached to one another by bonds that are not easily broken. Were different denominations to come together

"Around one common Mercy-Seat,"

and pour out in union their supplications to their common Father, through their common Mediator, we might rationally expect that many of the obstacles to a fairer understanding and to closer fellowship would be removed. Who, then, more appropriately than ourselves, can make advances, in the spirit of Christian love, towards a measure from which the happiest results may be anticipated? [1]

[1] The year 1858 will long be remembered as a period of "Union Prayer Meetings," and history will record results of a marked character. God has signally manifested his approbation of such fraternity.

I never heard an objection to union for such a purpose that did not contain internal evidence of its origin in a narrow, jealous, unlovely sectarian spirit. But whatever may be the barriers in the way of a general union for prayer, it certainly is possible for us as individuals to cultivate the habit of supplication for all Christians. The godly in all sects can pray, they do pray, for one another, saying from the heart, "Grace be with all them that love our Lord Jesus Christ in sincerity." Bishop Burgess, speaking of the desirableness of a fuller public recognition of one another as Christians, says: "I ask no other acknowledgment than that which is made by each in his secret chamber, in his private conversation, in his prayers for all who profess and call themselves Christians; and in his hopes of union hereafter with just men made perfect." Setting out of the account the blessings which may descend upon others in answer to such prayers, we may be sure that to those who offer them will accrue no small advantage. When Job offered prayer for those with whom he had been disputing, and by whose reproaches he had been deeply wounded, his captivity was turned, and the smile of heaven rested again on his tabernacle. Many a Christian has found deliverance from the bonds of spiritual gloom, and had his feet set in a large place, the moment he has sacrificed the selfishness of his prayers, and sincerely prayed for all Christians as the objects of his fervent affection. "Pray for the peace of Jerusalem; they shall prosper that love thee." How much of this kind of prayer there may be in secret is known only to Him who seeth in secret; but we know full well that our public devotions are not overburdened with it. Occasionally from the pulpit is heard a petition "for Christians of every name;" but seldom is there anything to indicate earnestness in the request. It is one of a stereotyped series, beginning with "all that are in authority," and ending with "thine ancient people the Jews." You, my brother, have heard language in prayer, that showed a prudent regard to some system of divinity, by the introduction of a conditional clause: "Do thou bless all denominations *so far as they have the truth.*" How considerate to define the limits within which God may consistently bestow his favor! Is He in danger of countenancing error by blessing those who hold it?

Were I addressing one of a different spirit from yourself, I would say, Let us pray more for all who are "the children of God by faith in Christ Jesus." In all our private devotions, let us take their case as well as our own to the footstool of mercy, and let us there espouse it as our own, and feel that in the success of our suit important results are involved. Let us pray for others before we pray for ourselves, and let our plea for them be as long, as particular, as urgent, as the plea for ourselves. When we surround the domestic altar, let us remember all Christians, and devoutly entreat the same gracious benedictions upon the entire "household of faith." In the place of social prayer, that "scene where spirits blend," let us not fail to implore "the God of all grace" to bestow upon all his children "the fulness of the blessing of the gospel of Christ." In the public sanctuary, let not the occupant of the pulpit, as he leads the devotions of his people, contract his or their desires for the Divine favor to the narrowness of a sect; but let him enlarge the solicitudes of his heart, and open his mouth wide, and make "supplication for all saints," and plead for the holiness, the usefulness, the happiness of all who love the Lord. The effect of such a service upon ourselves will assuredly be conservative and healing. And were we to know that others are in like manner praying for us, should we not feel our hearts drawn out towards them? And when we might meet them, should we not extend to them a warmer hand, and cast upon them a more confiding look of brotherly love? And would not they and we be in the best of all moods for a candid examination of the grounds of our difference?[1]

7. WE MAY ENCOURAGE A PACIFIC MINISTRY.

"Blessed are the peace-makers, for they shall be called the sons of God." This is one of the first lessons which the Great Teacher gave to his theological pupils, the future ministers of his Church. This lesson they thoroughly learned from his varied teachings and illustrative examples; with its spirit they were deeply impregnated; under its influence they proceeded to every department of their labor, seeking everywhere to promote peace both between man and his God, and between man and his fellow-man. Theirs was peculiarly "the ministry of reconciliation," and with commendable fidelity they executed their trust. We have but to read the narrative of their labors, as recorded in the Acts of the Apostles, and the

[1] At a late meeting of colporteurs, an Episcopal clergyman,—Rev. Dr. Johns, of Baltimore,—speaking of "an excessive denominationalism," said: "Wherever this goes beyond love for souls, something is wrong. So fearful am I of this spirit, that I have been accustomed for years, in passing a house of worship of some other denomination than my own, to lift my heart to God in prayer for that minister and his people." How Christlike that spirit! Would that there were more of it!

letters which they addressed to communities and to individuals, in order to discover how pacific was their spirit, how anxious they were for the prevalence of love and concord, and how keenly they felt when there appeared the least indication of schism or disunion. It would be a profitable service for any minister of Christ to analyze the Epistles with special reference to this one point, — the peace-loving disposition of the primitive ministry. He would be surprised to find how frequently, how strongly, and in what a variety of forms, "the elders" and "all the holy brethren" are exhorted, entreated, commanded to cultivate mutual affection, and to guard against everything that might tend to grieve and alienate and divide. In the letters to Timothy and Titus, especially, he would find counsels pertaining to this department well worthy to be considered by himself and by all who, as the messengers of "the Prince of Peace," are appointed to preach and to exemplify "the Gospel of Peace;" — counsels which clearly indicate that it was an original design of the ministry to preserve in the Church good-will and undisturbed harmony, as well as sound doctrine and faithful discipline. And how plain, how severe, are the remarks of the Apostles with respect to those self-willed and contentious teachers who pervert their facilities for promoting peace to opportunities for kindling strife and inflaming hatred! "From such turn away."

The Church has largely experienced both good and ill from the men whom she has received as her spiritual advisers and guides. The confidence reposed in them as the accredited representatives of Christ, the sacredness of their office, the knowledge of Divine things which they are supposed to possess, and the freedom of intercourse with the people to which they are generally welcomed, all contribute to their influence in determining the principles, and moulding the characters, and tempering the spirit, and directing the conduct, of the great mass of professed disciples. It will not be denied that they have often employed this influence in fomenting "discord among brethren," in aggravating the ferocity of party spirit, in rearing higher and stronger the separating barriers, in rendering the separated more belligerent and more implacable. With them commenced the first schisms that disfigured and crippled the Church. By them mainly have schisms been multiplied, and widened, and deepened, and perpetuated. They have been the guardian sentinels, posted along the lines of party entrenchments, to superintend their integrity, and, whenever invasion is threatened, to give the trumpet a *certain* sound. Jerome, one of the Christian Fathers, has these words:

"Searching the ancient histories, I can find none who have more rent the Church of God than those who sustained the office of ministers." Martin Luther is said often to have prayed: "From vain-glorious doctors, contentious pastors, and unprofitable questions, good Lord, deliver us."

The religious controversies which have inflicted so many wounds upon Christianity and upon Christian consciences, have generally been commenced and continued by factious ministers. No others could or would have originated or maintained them. Common Christians had no interest in them, and felt a repugnance to them, except so far as they became partisans and sympathized with their guides. Let the people of the United States interpret for themselves our Constitution, one of the plainest documents in the English language, and they would understand it alike. Their leaders misdirect them, and draw them off into parties rallied around some unintelligible, abstract construction, and teach them to regard one another as the enemies of their country and the generators of all political mischief. So, if the Bible, no part of which is "of any private interpretation," had been put into the hands of all Christians, and kept there, and they had been properly instructed to read and interpret it for themselves, the Church, we may believe, would never have been disturbed and harassed with those subtle distinctions and endless logomachies which have so grievously torn her own vitals, and often made her despicable in the eyes of unbelievers. Ecclesiastical History tells a most humiliating tale of centuries, with respect to the spirit and behaviour of a large portion of the Christian priesthood, their ambition, their contentiousness, their acrimony of spirit, their disregard of all courtesy, their inflammability of temper, their violence of denunciation, their bitterness of invective, their ingenuity in belligerent tactics, their rage for party victory; and to such men — demons they would in any other relation be called — may chiefly be traced the divisions and the hostile feelings and attitudes of the various sects which have successively appeared, and, like the renowned controvertists of Kilkenny, disappeared.

The minister of the gospel, especially the pastor of a Church, occupies a post of influence, and it is in his power to do much either for peace or for war, according to the end which he proposes to accomplish, the means he employs, and the spirit by which he is moved. He can promote good-will and harmony, or he can excite disaffection, and drive the divided farther asunder. He can be a fountain of bland influences that shall soothe and heal, or he can be a volcano pouring forth sulphureous elements that scorch and blacken and devastate.

Can we for a moment hesitate respecting the character and the spirit which we ought to encourage in the ministry of the Church? Have we any pleasure in the labors of a man who makes the pulpit the vehicle of inflammatory appeals, and who never seems to be better pleased than when he sees that he has propagated his own spirit, and kindled in other bosoms the flame that has charred his own? Is he the pastor for us who is fond of irritating other denominations by pungent witticisms, and sarcastic ridicule, and then applying the fiery caustic to the excoriated surface to see how the victims will writhe and scowl? Is he our preferred spiritual guide who, instead of leading us into green pastures and beside the still waters, conducts us into the sectarian battle-field where hearts bleed and love weeps?

If there be a spot on earth where the spirit of peace and love should have its cherished home, it is the pulpit. If there be a man on earth who ought to be baptized in that spirit, it is the minister of Jesus. It is good to come near to such a pulpit, sacred to Love, and to find it occupied by such a minister, "full of the Holy Ghost and of faith." It is good to pass our Sabbath hours in a sanctuary where there is a Calvary, and on that Calvary a Cross around which we may gather in humility, repentance, confession, faith and hope, and by the power of which we may feel ourselves drawn together somewhat in likeness of heavenly companionship. And it is good to be led to that Cross by a pastor who dwells near it himself, and breathes the atmosphere that surrounds it, and walks in the light that it pours upon the humble, and speaks the sentiments that it inspires, and prays like Him who bled upon it and gave it all its glory. He preaches the truth as he derives it for himself directly from the Word of God; but he does it without bigotry or dogmatism. "Set for the defence of the gospel," he "contends earnestly for the faith once delivered to the saints;" but he does it not factiously or provokingly. He warns all wrong-doers of "the wrath to come;" but he mingles with the holy wrath of God no wrath of his own. If he uses hard arguments, his words are soft. He is "patient towards all men," "gentle unto all men," "in meekness instructing those that oppose themselves." As "the servant of God," he does not "strive," and he stirs no strife among others. He is never satirical, except against immorality. Against persons he utters no reproachful epithets. He inflicts no unnecessary wounds. For the sake of peace, he yields everything except truth and conscience. He is more concerned for the progress of the general cause than for sectarian victory; for the salvation of souls than for the increase of his denomination. He dwells more upon the spiritual than the ritual of religion; more upon the fundamental than the circumstantial. He puts truths and duties in apostolic order and apostolic proportion, and insists upon each, in the apostolic spirit, according to its relative importance. He diffuses everywhere, and by every appropriate means, the genial and sunny influences of that heaven-born Charity which "suffereth long and is kind, envieth not, vaunteth not itself, is not puffed up, behaveth not unseemly, seeketh not her own, is not easily provoked, thinketh no evil, rejoiceth not in iniquity, but rejoiceth in the truth; beareth all things, believeth all things, hopeth all things, endureth all things," and "never faileth." He possesses and exhibits, in large measure, the wisdom that is "first pure, then peaceable, gentle, easy to be entreated, full of mercy and good fruits, without partiality and without hypocrisy." In him are blended two characteristics; he is wise as a serpent, harmless as a dove. He studies to promote brotherly love, regarding it as a proof of discipleship, and as adapted to convince unbelievers of the excellence of the gospel. Hence he exhorts all to be "kindly affectioned one to another," "forbearing one another in love." He finds the Church "wounded and half dead," and he pours in oil and wine, and endeavors to soothe her feverish throbbings with the healing hand of kindness. He labors to draw off the minds of the people from undue attention to inferior matters by presenting great truths for their contemplation, great commands for their obedience; and thus, like a wise physician, he skilfully administers the proper moral alteratives. In private prayer he wrestles with God for the peace and unity of the Church; in public devotion he pleads for the removal of the barriers that obstruct the free and holy fellowship of all believers. Like the High Priest of Israel, he never enters the holy place for the purpose of intercession, without the names of all the tribes upon his breast-plate. As the tabernacle was the rallying point of the host in its marches to Canaan, and the central bond of union around which was every nightly encampment, so this leader of a Christian flock plants the Cross in the centre, and invites all to encircle it in close combination, knowing for a certainty that there the spirit of discord cannot develop itself, — there every schismatical feeling must wither and die. He dwells much upon the oneness of God's people, having one Father, one Saviour, one hope, one inheritance. He is "a lover of good men," a lover of all goodness. For controversy he has no taste. As instinctively as the dove-like Spirit, he

"Flies from the realms of noise and strife."

He delights to work upon that part of the spiritual temple where the sound of axe and hammer is not heard. His great object is the conversion of sinners and their culture in holiness, and in all he has supreme reference to the glory of Christ, preferring rather to jewel the Redeemer's crown than his own. He anticipates with strong rapture the period when the whole Body of Christ shall be "compacted together in love," and "come into the unity of the faith;" the halcyon days of prophecy, when the godly seed shall rise above the partition walls by which they are divided, and flow together to certify, in the embrace of Christian fellowship, before the face of the world, the ancient power of godliness. He longs for the key-note to be struck, to which ten thousand times ten thousand voices shall respond in sweetest harmony, and to which angels themselves shall lend a delighted ear, finding in it the echo of their own on that day when they sang at the advent of the Redeemer. He is not widely known to the world;

he aspires not to the distinctions that men confer. His immediate influence is not far-reaching, but it is all healthful, and will go on through numerous channels, diffusing the beauty of holiness long after he shall have gone to his rest and his reward.

How benign is the influence of such a pastor! How green is the spot which he cultivates! How refreshing to place one's moral nature under such influences! How profitable to be trained by such a teacher for usefulness and heaven, himself leading the way! How great the pleasure of contributing to the support of such a minister, knowing that we are sustaining an agent of good, and good of the highest order! His less tolerant brethren may suspect him of favoring some heresy, or of abating his zeal for the truth; but none of these things move him. He believes that holiness and peace are inseparable concomitants, and that by promoting either he facilitates the advancement of the other. Like Chillingworth, he says, "If the ruptures of the Church might be composed, I do heartily wish that the cement might be made of my heart's blood;" or, like Baxter: "I can as willingly be a martyr for Love as for any article of my creed."

Were all the ministers even of one denomination thus to feel and act, would the cause of truth suffer in their hands? Would their Master rebuke, or commend them? How long would it be before the prejudices of others would melt away like snow in a summer atmosphere, and the thousands of divided Israel reünite under the peaceful standard of the Son of David? Prophecy has sketched the picture, "a thing of beauty," on the future, and blessed are they to whom it shall be "a joy forever." "The watchmen shall lift up the voice; with the voice TOGETHER shall they sing; for they shall SEE EYE TO EYE, when the Lord shall bring again Zion."

"Were love, in these the world's last doting years,
As frequent as the want of it appears,
The churches warmed, they would no longer hold
Such frozen figures, stiff as they are cold;
Relenting forms would lose their power, or cease,
And e'en the dipped and sprinkled live in peace;
Each heart would quit its prison in the breast,
And flow in free communion with the rest."[1]

8. WE MAY PATRONIZE A PEACE-MAKING PRESS.

The alienations and animosities among religious people are aggravated in no small degree by the newspapers, magazines, and reviews, which they read and support. These publications are now, what the pulpit once was, the principal arena of

[1] William Cowper.

sectarian debate. There the pugnacious hide themselves behind the editorial impersonality or the fictitious signature, and carry on a warfare which contributes far more to the embittering of disaffection than to the evolving of truth or the maintaining of right. An editor inflames the minds of his readers, and the readers become correspondents, at once encouraging the editor and exasperating the inflammation in their own bosoms; and thus the process goes on, reciprocally multiplying and envenoming its pernicious tendencies.

Does any one doubt the power of the periodical press to evoke or allay the unchristian spirit? Let him habitually read two religious newspapers, differing in their tone and temper, — the one kind, courteous, fraternal towards all denominations of Christians; the other controversial, fault-finding, sarcastic, — and, if he will carefully observe the effect upon his own sensitiveness, he will soon be able to bear unequivocal testimony to the wide difference of their tendencies. The former will ever come like an excellent oil that soothes, refreshes, and perfumes his inner soul; while every sheet of the other will be to his feelings like a corrosive cataplasm, blistering whatever it touches. The one promotes a spirit of love and genial union; the other a spirit of irritability, jealousy and contention. The one strengthens the bonds of Christian attachment; the other harshly ruptures the social ligaments, and incapacitates them for reünion.

As lovers of peace and harmony, we may direct our whole influence in favor of a press whose issues are eminently Christian. We may keep far away from ourselves and our families the publications that indulge in sneers at other denominations, and captious criticisms, and satirical thrusts, and ungenerous insinuations; we may welcome those — and such there are — that inculcate sound opinions in a lovely spirit, striving to tranquillize the perturbed elements, and to cultivate those feelings and habits which shall bring nearer together the separated flock of Christ. Happy indeed will be the day when all writers shall be peace-makers in Zion, and when all their readers shall be lovers and promoters of Christian Brotherhood.

9. WE MAY IMPLORE A LARGER EFFUSION OF THE HOLY SPIRIT.

"There is one Body and one Spirit." So said an inspired Apostle; and in his day there was nothing even in appearance to contradict the assertion, or to render doubtful its correctness. The whole company of believers was that one Body. Though composed of a diversity of members, yet they were all so arranged and "fitly framed together," as to constitute one compact, symmetrical whole, of which Christ was the intelligent, controlling Head. In this Body there was one Spirit, and that the Holy Spirit, which dwelt there as the animating, assimilating, combining Principle. So long as the Spirit inhabited that Body as the indwelling Life, the Body remained united. When the Spirit departed, then the Body began at once to exhibit signs of decomposition, and where the carcass was, there the eagles were gathered together. From that time to the present the deficiency of spiritual life in the Church has been the chief preventive to the reünion of her separated elements. When the scattered fragments of a man came together in the valley of vision, they were skilfully combined into a perfect form. But had not the Breath entered that form and given it animation, it would soon have dissolved and become as unsightly as before. So the portions of the divided Church may be brought into contact, and by mechanical forces made to assume the appearance of unity; but, without the indwelling Spirit, all will go to pieces again, and be more remote than ever from that living unity which was once its beauty and glory.

If, therefore, we desire to see Christians united and happily coöperating as the members of one Body, enlivened by one Spirit, we must, in God's appointed way, secure the return of that grieved and alienated Agent by whom alone the work can be accomplished. He only can counteract that antagonist agent which has usurped his place and reigned as the spirit of division and death.

In all ages, just so far as Christians have enjoyed the presence and the fulness of the Spirit, have they been divested of the sectarian element, and diligently sought for some common basis upon which they could stand side by side evincing to the world their oneness in Christ Jesus. And in our day, there is among all the more spiritual members of every denomination a strong tendency towards a greater union. When a religious revival commences in a place, how common is it to see Christians of different names rush together, praying and laboring as if there were no differences of opinion or interest. The secret of this affectionate coöperation is found in the presence of the Holy Spirit, whose power has weakened sectarian repulsion, and given increased activity to Christian attraction. When this extraordinary Influence is withdrawn, how often do we see the different denominations returning to their respective inclosures, and commencing a most unlovely course of conduct! Instead of endeavoring to nurse and instruct the converts, they seem, by the efforts which they make, and the artifices they employ, to be intent upon nothing so much as to secure the largest possible number to swell their own denominational triumph! Their union in the first instance made a powerful impression upon the community, and facilitated the progress of the good work; and their union was sincere, for it was the product of the Divine Spirit. But the subsequent competitions and conflicts of partisan interests, stirred up by the agent of all evil, sickened the community, and fastened a new stigma upon revivals.

The Spirit of God is not wholly absent from any of Christ's genuine disciples. Every Christian is a temple of the Holy Ghost. Every evangelical denomination is favored with the visits and the benedictions of the blessed Comforter. Consequently, all Christians have some points of resemblance, and some love one to another. But they have not enough of the Spirit to make that resemblance complete, or to produce that mutual affection which would bind them indissolubly together.

To this point, then, we ought to direct our immediate and earnest attention. The great want of the Church universal is ours, — the want of a large measure of the Divine Influence. The Holy Spirit is preëminently the "Repairer of the breach, the Restorer of paths to dwell in," and his presence and efficacious operations are everywhere imperatively needed. Let us take right views of this necessity, and open our hearts as well as our understandings to the full force of the conviction, that for all spiritual improvement we are dependent on the sanctifying agency of the Holy Spirit. And let us pray for an enlarged effusion of that Spirit — the needed blessing, and the one which Christ has specially promised to all who ask it. Let us pray more, and pray better. Let us be such in character and spirit and motive, as that we may have power with God; and prevail. Let us go alone and pray that the Spirit may return to us and to all Christians in his fulness; that he may descend into every one of our hearts as the purifying flame, and consume all the unholiness of our natures, and that thus we may be individually prepared for the great process of Christian consolidation. Let us unite with all who love the Saviour, to pray; and, while we endeavor to unite in the service upon Christian principles and for Christian ends, let us lay our hearts together before the throne, and call down upon them the only Influence that can melt and blend them into One.

VALUABLE WORKS

PUBLISHED BY

GOULD AND LINCOLN,

59 WASHINGTON STREET, BOSTON.

SACRED RHETORIC: Or, Composition and Delivery of Sermons. By HENRY J. RIPLEY, Prof. in Newton Theological Institution. Including Ware's Hints on Extemporaneous Preaching. Second thousand. 12mo, 75 cts.

An admirable work, clear and succinct in its positions, and well supported by a variety of reading and illustrations. — *N. Y. Literary World.*

We have looked over this work with a lively interest. It is will command readers, being a comprehensive manual of great practical utility. — *Phil. Ch. Chronicle.*

The author contemplates a man *preparing to compose a discourse*; and unfolds to him the process through which his mind ought to pass. We commend the work to ministers, and to those preparing for the sacred office. — *Phil. Ch. Observer.*

It presents a rich variety of rules for the practical use of clergymen, and evinces the good sense, the large experience, and the excellent spirit of Dr. Ripley. The volume is well fitted to instruct and stimulate the writer of sermons. — *Bibliotheca Sacra.*

It is not a compilation, but is an original treatise, fresh, practical, and comprehensive, and adapted to the pulpit offices of the present day. It is full of valuable suggestions, and abounds with clear illustrations. — *Zion's Herald.*

It cannot be too frequently perused by those whose duty it is to *persuade.* — *Cong.*

His canons on selecting texts, stating the proposition, collecting and arranging materials, style, delivery, etc., are just, and well stated. — *Ch. Mirror.*

It is pervaded by a manly tone, and abounds in judicious counsels; it is compactly written and admirably arranged, both for study and reference. — *N. Y. Recorder.*

THE CHRISTIAN WORLD UNMASKED. By JOHN BERRIDGE, A. M., Vicar of Everton, Bedfordshire, Chaplain to the Right Hon. The Earl of Buchan, etc. *New Edition.* With Life of the Author, by the REV. THOMAS GUTHRIE, D. D., Minister of Free St. John's, Edinburgh. 16mo, cloth.

"The book," says DR. GUTHRIE, in his Introduction, "which we introduce anew to the public, has survived the test of years, and still stands towering above things of inferior growth like a cedar of Lebanon. Its subject is all important; in doctrine it is sound to the core; it glows with fervent piety; it exhibits a most skilful and unsparing dissection of the dead professor; while its style is so remarkable, that he who could *preach* as Berridge has *written*, would hold any congregation by the ears."

THE CHRISTIAN REVIEW. Edited by Prof. JAMES D. KNOWLES, BARNAS SEARS, and S. F. SMITH. 8 vols. Commencing with vol. one. Half cl., lettered, 8,00.

Single volumes, (except the first,) may be had in numbers, 1,00.

These first eight volumes of the Christian Review contain valuable contributions from the leading men of the Baptist and several other denominations, and will be found a valuable acquisition to any library.

DR. WILLIAMS'S WORKS.

RELIGIOUS PROGRESS; Discourses on the Development of the Christian Character. By WILLIAM R. WILLIAMS, D. D. Third edition. 12mo, cloth, 85 cts.

This work is from the pen of one of the brightest lights of the American pulpit. We scarcely know of any living writer who has a finer command of powerful thought and glowing, impressive language than he. — DR. SPRAGUE, *Albany Atlas.*

This book is a rare phenomenon in these days. It is a rich exposition of Scripture, with a fund of practical religious wisdom, conveyed in a style so strong and massive as to remind one of the English writers of two centuries ago; and yet it abounds in fresh illustrations drawn from every (even the latest opened) field of science and of literature. — *Methodist Quarterly.*

His power of apt illustration is without a parallel among modern writers. The mute pages spring into life beneath the magic of his radiant imagination, but never at the expense of solidity of thought or strength of argument. — *Harpers' Monthly.*

Every page radiant with "thoughts that burn," leave their indelible impression upon the mind. — *N. Y. Com. Adv.*

The strength and compactness of argumentation, the correctness and beauty of style, and the importance of the animating idea, place them among the most finished homiletic productions of the day. — *N. Y. Evangelist.*

Dr. Williams has no superior among American divines. He seems familiar with the literature of the world, and lays his vast resources under contribution to illustrate and adorn every theme which he investigates. We wish the volume could be placed in every religious family in the country. — *Phil. Ch. Chronicle.*

LECTURES ON THE LORD'S PRAYER. Third ed. 85c.

We welcome this volume as a valuable contribution to our literature — *Ch. Wit.*

In reading, we resolved to mark the passages which we most admired, but soon found that we should be obliged to mark nearly all of them. — *Ch. Secretary.*

It bears in every page the mark of an elegant writer and an accomplished scholar, an acute reasoner and a cogent moralist. Some passages are so decidedly eloquent that we instinctively find ourselves looking round as if upon an audience, and ready to join them with audible applause — *Ch. Inquirer.*

We are reminded of the old English writers, whose vigorous thought, and gorgeous imagery, and varied learning, have made their writings an inexhaustible mine for the scholars of the present day. — *Ch. Observer.*

Among the very best homiletical efforts of the age. — *Ch. Parlor Mag.*

MISCELLANIES. Improved edition. *(Price reduced.)* 1,25.

☞ This work, which has been heretofore published in octavo form at 1,75 per copy, is published by the present proprietors in one handsome 12mo volume, at the low price of 1,25.

Dr. Williams is a profound scholar and a brilliant writer. — *N. Y. Evangelist.*

The natural expression of a mind teeming with the "spoils of time" and the treasures of study in almost every department of learning. -- *N. Y. Tribune.*

A delightful volume. — *Methodist Review.*

Glad to see this volume. We wish such men abounded in every sect. — *Ch. Reg.*

One of the richest volumes that has been given to the public for years. — *Bap. Reg.*

WORKS BY JOHN ANGELL JAMES.

THE CHURCH IN EARNEST. 18mo, cloth, 50 cts.

Mr. James's writings all have one object, to do execution. He writes under impulse — "Do something, *do it.*" He aims to raise the standard of piety, holiness in the heart, and holiness of life. The influence of this work must be highly salutary. — *Puritan Recorder.*

Let it be scattered like autumn leaves. We believe its perusal will do much to convince and arouse the Christian. The reader will feel that he is called into the Church of Christ, not to enjoy only, but to labor. - *N. Y. Recorder.*

Purchase a number of copies of this work, and lend them and keep them in circulation *till they are worn out! — Mothers' Assistant.*

Probably no writer of the present age has done so much to promote the interests of vital and practical religion as Mr. James. This work should be in the hands of every professor. — *Congregational Journal.*

A more important work could not be presented to the world. – *Bap. Memorial.*

This new work of Mr. James points out the nature and effects of earnest piety with reference to individual action for the promotion of one's personal religion, the salvation of others, the religion of the family, and of the church. No time should be lost in putting it into the hands of church members. — *Ch. Mirror, Portland.*

"Its arguments and appeals are well adapted to prompt to action. We trust it will be universally read." — *N. Y. Observer.*

To give the work a word of approbation, were but a poor tribute. It should receive the earnest attention of Christians of every name. — *Southern Lit. Gazette.*

CHRISTIAN PROGRESS; a Sequel to "The Anxious Inquirer after Salvation." 18mo, cloth, 30 cts.

None of the works of James's (all of them of uncommon practical excellence) are better calculated for circulation among the churches than this. It ought to be sold by hundreds of thousands, until every church member in the land has bought, read, marked, learned, and inwardly digested. — *Congregationalist.*

To every lover of progressive holiness, we commend this volume. — *Ch. Secretary.*

So eminently is it adapted to do good, that we feel no surprise that it should make one of the publishers' excellent publications. It exhibits the whole subject of growth in grace and guards the young Christian against many mistakes, into which he is in danger of falling. — *Puritan Recorder.*

Mr. James has rendered himself one of the most popular and useful writers of the day. — *Zion's Advocate.*

It is written as a sequel to the anxious inquirer, "whose praise is in all the churches." The subject is one of equal importance, and the author addresses himself with characteristic ardor and success to the theme. — *Southern Baptist.*

CHURCH MEMBER'S GUIDE. Edited by the Rev. J. Overton Choules, D. D. New Edition. With an Introductory Essay, by the Rev. Hubbard Winslow. Cloth, 33 cts.

The spontaneous effusion of our heart, on laying the book down, was, — may every church member in our land possess this book. — *Christian Secretary.*

A pastor writes, "I sincerely wish that every professor of religion in the land may possess this excellent manual. I am anxious that every member of my church should possess it, and shall be happy to promote its circulation." **Kk**

IMPORTANT WORK.

KITTO'S POPULAR CYCLOPÆDIA OF BIBLICAL LITERATURE. Condensed from the larger work. By the Author, JOHN KITTO, D. D., Author of "Scripture Daily Readings," &c. Assisted by JAMES TAYLOR, D. D. With *over* 500 *Illustrations.* 3,00.

This work is designed to furnish a DICTIONARY OF THE BIBLE, embodying the products of the best and most recent researches in biblical literature, in which the scholars of Europe and America have been engaged. The work, the result of immense labor and research, is pronounced, by universal consent, the best work of its class extant. It is not only intended for *ministers* and *theological students*, but is also particularly adapted to *parents, Sabbath school teachers, and the great body of the religious public.* The *illustrations*, amounting to *more than* 300, are of the highest order.

A condensed view of the various topics comprehended in the work.

1. BIBLICAL CRITICISM, — Embracing the History of the Bible Languages; Canon of Scripture; Literary History and Peculiarities of the Sacred Books; Formation and History of Scripture Texts.

2. HISTORY, — Proper Names of Persons; Biographical Sketches of prominent Characters; Detailed Accounts of important Events recorded in Scripture; Chronology and Genealogy of Scripture.

3. GEOGRAPHY, — Names of Places; Description of Scenery; Boundaries and Mutual Relations of the Countries mentioned in Scripture, so far as necessary to illustrate the Sacred Text.

4. ARCHÆOLOGY, — Manners and Customs of the Jews and other nations mentioned in Scripture; their Sacred Institutions, Military Affairs, Political Arrangements, Literary and Scientific Pursuits.

5. PHYSICAL SCIENCE, — Scripture Cosmogony and Astronomy, Zoology, Mineralogy, Botany, Meteorology.

In addition to numerous flattering notices and reviews, personal letters from *a large number of the most distinguished Ministers and Laymen of different religious denominations in the country* have been received, highly commending this work as admirably adapted to ministers, Sabbath school teachers, heads of families, and *all* Bible students.

The following extract of a letter is a fair specimen of individual letters received from *each* of the gentlemen whose names are given below: —

"I have examined it with special and unalloyed satisfaction. It has the rare merit of being all that it professes to be; and very few, I am sure, who may consult it will deny that, in richness and fulness of detail, it surpasses their expectation. Many ministers will find it a valuable auxiliary; but its chief excellence is, that it furnishes just the facilities which are needed by the thousands in families and Sabbath schools, who are engaged in the important business of biblical education. It is in itself a library of reliable information."

W. B. Sprague, D. D., Albany; J. J. Carruthers, D. D., Portland; Joel Hawes, D. D., Hartford, Ct.; Daniel Sharp, D. D., Boston; N. L. Frothingham, D. D., Boston; Ephraim Peabody, D. D., Boston; A. L. Stone, Boston; John S. Stone, D. D., Brooklyn; J. B. Waterbury, D. D., Boston; Baron Stow, D. D., Boston; Thomas H. Skinner, D. D., New York; Samuel W. Worcester, D. D., Salem; Horace Bushnell, D. D., Hartford, Ct.; Right Reverend J. M. Wainwright, D. D., New York; Gardner Spring, D. D., New York; W. T. Dwight, D. D., Portland; E. N. Kirk, Boston; Prof. George Bush, author of "Notes on the Scriptures," New York; Howard Malcom, D. D., author of "Bible Dictionary;" Henry J. Ripley, D. D., author of "Notes on the Scriptures;" N. Porter, Prof. in Yale College, New Haven, Ct.; Jared Sparks, Edward Everett, Theodore Frelinghuysen, Robert C. Winthrop, John McLean, Simon Greenleaf, Thomas S. Williams, — and a large number of others of like character and standing of the above, whose names cannot here appear. H

www.ingramcontent.com/pod-product-compliance
Lightning Source LLC
LaVergne TN
LVHW011206110826
845150LV00006B/1339